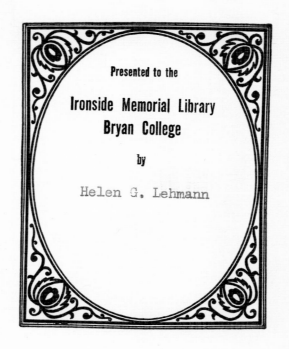

PENNY ❧

Other Books by Hal Borland

The Outdoors

AN AMERICAN YEAR
THE ENDURING PATTERN
BEYOND YOUR DOORSTEP
SUNDIAL OF THE SEASONS
COUNTRYMAN: A SUMMARY OF BELIEF
OUR NATURAL WORLD (Editor)
HILL COUNTRY HARVEST
HOMELAND: A REPORT FROM THE COUNTRY
BORLAND COUNTRY

People and Places

THIS HILL, THIS VALLEY
HIGH, WIDE AND LONESOME
THE DOG WHO CAME TO STAY

Fiction

THE SEVENTH WINTER
THE AMULET
WHEN THE LEGENDS DIE
KING OF SQUAW MOUNTAIN

Folklore

ROCKY MOUNTAIN TIPI TALES
THE YOUNGEST SHEPHERD

Poetry

AMERICA IS AMERICANS

HAL BORLAND

PENNY

The Story of a Free-Soul Basset Hound

With drawings by
TAYLOR OUGHTON

J. B. LIPPINCOTT COMPANY
Philadelphia & New York

U. S. Library of Congress Cataloging in Publication Data

Borland, Hal Glen, birth date
   Penny; the story of a free-soul basset hound.

   SUMMARY: The author recounts his experiences with a stray
basset hound.
     1. Basset-hounds—Legends and stories. [1. Basset hounds]
I. Oughton, Taylor, birth date II. Title.
QL795.D6B63   818'.5'207   74–37927
ISBN–0–397–00864–3

First edition
Printed in the United States of America

For **BARBARA**

She gave her heart.

PENNY ⟞

One ◆

It was March, with a foot of snow on the ground, and we were hungry for spring. It was only two more weeks till the vernal equinox, and change was inevitable; but we wanted warm days and opening buds and singing birds. This day had started out cold again, with no sign of that thaw we wanted. I went out after breakfast and filled the bird feeders again, for the chickadees and tree sparrows were parading their hunger, the chicks coming to the kitchen window and as much as demanding a handout. So I filled the feeders and came back indoors and we started going over the market list. I had a couple of errands in the village and might as well do the marketing while I was there. And Barbara glanced out the window and asked, "Whose dog is that?"

I looked and saw a black and tan dog, long as a beagle but with even shorter legs and longer ears. It was standing in the snow beneath the old apple tree where I had just filled the bird feeders. "Darned if I know," I said. "Stranger to me." And I wondered why she is the one who always sees the unusual, the unexpected. Long ago I learned to look first when she says, "What's that out there?" and ask questions, if any, afterward. She saw the woodcock beside the woodshed and the wood duck in the apple tree. She saw the snowy owl in the pear tree not twenty feet from the window. She saw the wild turkeys out in the pasture, and the family of otters looping along the pasture fence on their way over the mountain from the river to Twin Lakes. Now I looked, then asked, "Why don't you ever see ordinary dogs, or birds?"

"Isn't that an ordinary dog?"

"Well, it *is* a dog, I'll admit that. But—"

"It's cute. What kind is it?"

"Looks like a basset hound, I'd say."

"Funny looking. What is a basset hound?"

"A hunting dog. Away back, in England, they used them to hunt badgers. Maybe that's where the name came from —badger, basset. I don't really know. Nowadays they hunt rabbits, like beagles. But their legs are so short they can't run very fast."

10

The strange dog was looking hopefully up at the suet can, hung from a wire in the apple tree. But it seemed to know there wasn't a chance of getting that suet. It turned and looked at the house. It had a face something like that of a bloodhound, but not so wrinkled. The tan and white markings on its face made it look almost clownish rather than sad. Bloodhounds always look sad and worried.

I looked at the market list again. "What does 'black puppie' mean? Spelled with 'ie' instead of 'y.' "

Barbara looked at the notation. "Black pepper," she said. "You've got dogs on your mind." We went through the list, I got my coat and when we looked out again the strange dog had disappeared. The furrow it had plowed in the snow—you couldn't call it a set of tracks; that short-legged dog almost had to swim through the snow—led around the house to the driveway and disappeared on the freshly plowed road. When I went out to the garage I looked up and down the road and saw no sign of a dog. Nor did I see any but the familiar dogs of our neighbors as I went to the village. That dog had vanished as though into thin air.

I did my errands and the marketing and came home, and the day went pretty much as usual. By midafternoon the sun went under a cloud cover and it turned chilly again, so instead of going for a walk we settled down to a game of Scrabble. About five-thirty Barbara went to the kitchen and put a pot of vegetable soup on to heat. On the way back to our game she passed the front door, paused there a moment and exclaimed, "Oh, here's your friend again."

I couldn't imagine which friend she meant. I got up and started to the door, and before I got there she opened it and in came the black and tan dog we had seen under the bird

11

feeders that morning. It came in head up, tail wagging, like an honored guest accepting hospitality. It didn't cringe or skulk or even hesitate. It came in expecting to have a great big welcome, maybe a speech and a banquet.

I stopped and stared, and it looked at me with those big brown eyes and a face that was absolutely self-possessed. It practically said, Here I am, you lucky people!

Barbara looked at me, and I said, "It's all yours. You let it in."

"I just opened the door and he *came* in! But he's hungry. You can see that. He probably hasn't had a thing to eat all day."

"So you want a dog, huh? You didn't tell me."

"No, I don't want a dog! This one isn't a tramp. Somebody owns him and probably is out looking for him right now. See, he even has a collar."

She was right. It had a red leather collar. I bent down to look at the license tag, but there wasn't any tag on the collar. The dog licked my hands. I lifted one long ear, then the other, looking for a tattoo mark that might identify it. There wasn't a mark. It was totally anonymous. I wondered why the owner of a dog obviously of good stock, by no means a mongrel, hadn't put some identification on it.

I stood up, and Barbara said, "I'm sure somebody owns him." She spoke to the dog. "Hungry? Want something to eat?" and the dog wagged enthusiastically, licked its chops.

"See! He's starved!"

"She," I said. "It's a bitch."

"All right, She. How about it, She? Come on," and Barbara led the way through the living room. The basset fol-

12

lowed, curious about everything but most mannerly, like a princess inspecting a strange hostelry. I was glad to see that she seemed to approve. They went through the hallway to the kitchen, and the basset saw the refrigerator. She went to it and stood waiting, obviously expecting Barbara to open it and work magic—produce marvelous things for a dog to eat. She knew refrigerators and what they meant.

"Something warm," Barbara said, "on a day like this," and she got out a carton of milk, poured a pint or so into a pan and set it to heat. The basset watched as she took an old bowl from the bowl closet, poured corn flakes into it and waited for the milk to warm. Then she asked me to bring a newspaper, put it on the floor in the enclosed back porch, poured the warm milk over the corn flakes and set the bowl out for the dog. The basset ate as though she had been starved for a week, licked the bowl clean, then went back to the kitchen. When she got no second helping she returned to the living room. We watched to see if she would try to climb onto the couch or the chairs, forbidden territory to any dogs in this house. She didn't. She explored the whole room, finally found the place she wanted and lay down on the rug under a bench that stood against the wall. She stretched out, sighed deeply, closed her eyes and settled into a nap, completely at home.

We closed the living room doors, went back to the kitchen and took trays and bowls of soup to the library. We talked as we ate. No, we agreed, we didn't want a dog. And we agreed that we hadn't just acquired a dog. We had done an act of charity, taken in a lost dog, warmed, fed and sheltered it for the night. If we couldn't find the owner in the next few hours we would find someone who knew where the dog belonged by tomorrow. A dog like that certainly would be reported missing.

When we finished eating I called my friend Dave, the local dog warden. No, Dave hadn't any report of a missing basset hound, but he would take a note of it. He asked about color, markings, any identification. We discussed bassets. Not many of them around, so it shouldn't be hard to locate the owner. Dave would be in touch.

Then I called the Little Guild of St. Francis, which cares for lost dogs and cats and finds homes for strays and waifs. No, they didn't have any report of a lost basset either. But if the owner didn't turn up they would be glad to take the dog and find a good home for it. Bassets were even-tempered, gentle around children. A little inclined to wander, but good pets for all that. And we, too, discussed bassets.

Finally I called the town clerk. It was after hours, so I called her at home. Lila issues dog licenses, and I hoped she would remember who in town owned a basset. But her memory wasn't that good, she said. Offhand, though, she couldn't think of anyone. However, she would check the records in the office tomorrow. Meanwhile, how had we been and what had we been doing? What were we going to do about this weather? We talked for ten minutes and hung up.

By then it was after nine o'clock and our bedtime. We decided that the dog could sleep on the enclosed kitchen porch. I got an old Navy blanket, folded it into a square and put it out there. The dog inspected it. She found nothing special to object to, but she made it quite clear that she would have preferred to sleep in the living room, under the

14

bench. You don't quarter visiting royalty on the kitchen porch, do you? Yes, we did.

But before lights out I took her outdoors and wondered if she might take off and be gone. She didn't. Not her! She wallowed about in the snow in the dooryard, found a place that suited her, did what she was supposed to do and came lunging back to me beside the kitchen door. And when told that she was going to sleep on the porch, positively, not maybe, she lay down on the blanket, looked at me with a lightly veiled air of annoyance, indicated that she would make the best of plebeian accommodations for the night, at least, and began to lick her legs dry. I closed the kitchen door, turned out the lights and went upstairs. To read in bed for an hour or so and then, if all was quiet, go to sleep.

All was quiet.

I was up as usual the next morning soon after five. The minute I reached the kitchen I heard the dog. She didn't bark, but she whined loud enough to be heard the first time. No barking. Simply a dignified but insistent demand that she be allowed admission to the bosom of the family. I opened the door to the porch and she was one big wiggle, tail to nose tip, and one big prance with those short, stocky legs and big feet. She danced, a rather elephantine dance, and gave me a greeting, less than a bark, more than a whine, a throaty kind of dog-talk that reminded me of the rather sultry, smoky voice of one of the better blues singers. She licked my hands, would have licked my face had I allowed it. I told her to calm down, not wake Barbara, contain herself and act like a grownup. She subsided somewhat, and while I set the coffee to perk for myself I warmed milk for her. I gave her a bowl of bread and milk, apologizing for the absence of anything more substantial. We hadn't been expecting canine guests, and we don't keep dog food on the pantry shelves as a general rule. She accepted both the apology and the bread and milk, and I assured her that she would be back home before the day was out and would undoubtedly have her share of the fatted calf. Then I closed the porch door and took my coffee to the library.

I settled down to read the previous day's *New York Times*. It comes by rural mail delivery around noon, gets a quick front-page glance and is left till the next morning for a real reading. News is news, I say, until I have heard or read it. I was back to the first sports page when the dog demanded further attention. She whined, and when that got no results she barked discreetly. Finally she barked insistently, and I let her into the kitchen and told her to shut up. She did shut up, but her spirits weren't so easily dampened. She frisked and pranced and did her best to entertain me. I wasn't in need of entertainment at that time of day and told her so rather firmly. She stopped prancing, and I returned to the library and my newspaper. She evidently explored the living room, found nothing there to amuse or entertain and finally came and lay down at my feet under the library table. What she wanted, apparently, was human company, and I couldn't begrudge her that. She lay quietly and I read my newspaper.

When Barbara came downstairs soon after six she got an even more eager welcome than I had. The dog danced on her hind legs, pawing at Barbara with those big forefeet. She had to be scolded down. "No! Not in this house. No! We don't like dogs who jump on people!" The dog seemed to understand. She stopped jumping and began playing cat —she rubbed Barbara's ankles, then slapped her legs with her tail, *whack-whack-whack*, until Barbara stopped *that*. And the dog sat down with a baffled, forlorn look, so sad that Barbara laughed at her. The laughter only inspired more prancing, though at a little distance, and a series of barks. Her voice was surprisingly low in pitch and full in volume, the bark of a dog twice as big. So that was one reason for that deep, broad chest—big lungs for a lot of voice.

She got another breakfast. Barbara fed her corn flakes before I knew she was doing it, and the dog lapped them up. Then she was put outdoors. She wallowed in the snow, shook herself and went out into the road. Then she vanished. I thought she was really gone this time, but half an hour later there she was at the door, whining to be let in.

As soon as it was a decent country hour to call people, eight-thirty around here, we began phoning again. I called my friend Morris, a fox hunter and hound-dog man who knows every dog for miles around. No, Morris said, he didn't know of anyone with a basset. Oh, wait a minute. A man over near Norfolk used to have one, but that was five or six years ago and the dog was an old dog then. No, he didn't know anyone with a young basset. Then he said, with a chuckle, "Maybe you've got yourself a rabbit hound again." He has been at me for five years to get another hound.

Barbara called the dog warden in the next village to the east, but he had no record of a missing basset. Then she called the postmaster in Ashley Falls, just over the line in Massachusetts. Christine is a personal friend, and she knows everybody in that area. Finally Barbara said, "Say that again." She listened, then she laughed, and she turned to me and said, "Try calling her Hannah."

"Calling who Hannah?"

17

"The dog!"

I tried. "Here, Hannah. Come, Hannah. Hannah, Hannah!" No response whatever.

Barbara said to Christine, "She doesn't seem to respond at all. Thanks anyway. 'Bye." And she turned to me. "Are you sure she doesn't know the name Hannah?"

"You try," I said.

Barbara tried. No reaction except a polite show of attention. Then I said, "Mary!" and the dog looked at me. I said, "Jane!" and got exactly the same response. Barbara said, "Hannah!" again, and we knew it was no use. Then Barbara told me about Hannah.

"The folks who live in the old Hardy place used to have a basset, but she wouldn't stay home. So they gave her to the cleaning woman who worked for them. She lives away over on Clayton Road, but the dog comes back to the Hardy place now and then, and of course that's only about three miles up the road from here. And," she finished the recital, "that dog is named Hannah."

"Good try," I said. "But I don't think we've got Hannah. Do you?"

"No."

Back to the phone. Barbara called all the neighbors. Nobody had—or knew anybody who had—a basset. But one neighbor said he had heard a missing-dog report on the Barrington radio that morning. A black and tan she-dog, as he called her, named Susie. We tried Susie on the dog in our living room. She wasn't Susie either, or if she was she wasn't admitting it.

So Barbara called the Barrington radio station, but the girl who answered said the missing-dog announcer had left the studio, she didn't know when he would be back and she didn't have his phone number. She was very sorry not to be of more assistance.

Then I took over, called the Barrington police department and got a sergeant there who evidently read my books. He listened to my questions, said, "Nope, no lost dogs of any breed. You've got a basset, they're a good dog. Keep her. Maybe you've got a dog to take old Pat's place." And that was that.

By then it was midmorning, and the dog decided she wanted to go out again. I opened the front door; she went out onto the front porch and stood there nosing the air. She went down the front steps, down the front walk, turned and looked at the house, then trotted up the road. We waited half an hour, but she didn't come back. Finally we got lunch and ate, and still there was no sign of the dog. Midafternoon and we went for a walk, up the road that winds beside the river. No sign of the basset, either on the road or at the house when we returned.

"Well," Barbara said, "I guess that is that. Just a transient who stopped in for a meal and a bed and didn't even say thank you."

"Easy come," I said, "easy go."

"All I wish," Barbara said, "is that we'd been able to find her owner. Somebody loves her. She has a home somewhere. I hate to see a nice dog like that, just go off like a common tramp dog. I'll bet some child is out looking for her right this minute."

"Yeah. Some child up in New Hampshire, probably. Or Canada. Nobody around here seems to have heard of her. She's a real wanderer, a *far* wanderer, that dog."

"She was well behaved. Somebody taught her manners."

We spent most of the evening listening for her at the door, though neither of us would have admitted it if we had been asked. But she evidently had gone her own way, and we didn't regret her going. We agreed on that, to each other. We weren't going to have another Pat on our hands.

Two ∾

Pat adopted us the first winter we lived here, almost twenty years ago. He and another dog simply arrived, total strangers to the area, and after a trial period— we, not the dogs, were on trial—they settled down to stay. Eventually we had to give the other dog away; he was a mischief-maker and a deer-chaser. But Pat stayed on, became a part of the family and, eventually, canine king of the valley. We never learned where he came from or what were his antecedents, but he apparently was a beagle-foxhound cross. He was the best rabbit dog anywhere around. He was a demon woodchuck hunter. He was in every sense an individual, a character. Eventually I wrote a book about him, *The Dog Who Came to Stay*, and Pat became a minor celebrity. Letters came for him and about him from all over this country and Europe. Mail meant nothing to him, of course, but visitors did, and readers from halfway across the continent came past just to see him. Pat became an absolute ham, lying on the front steps, waiting for the inevitable car to come drifting past. If someone shouted, "There he is! There's Pat!" he would look up and preen. If the car stopped he would stand up and pose. If someone produced a camera he would even strut down toward the car and allow his picture to be taken.

We never knew just how old he was, but we guessed he was at least twelve, maybe fourteen, when his book was published. He lived another year and a half, wearing his age like a badge, gray around the face, stiff in all the joints every morning, but never admitting, if he ever knew, that he was an old dog. Active till the end, he died peacefully, and we knew what a privilege it had been to know him. But we had no intention of ever having another dog. Our lives involve occasional trips, usually on business, and Pat hated to be left behind, disliked even the best of kennel keepers. Besides, we didn't think it would be fair either to us or to another dog to compare the new dog with Pat, as we inevitably would. So we said a firm no to those who insisted we must get a dog to replace Pat. But it took some time to make our friends and quite a few friendly but unknown readers accept our decision and stop urging very special puppies on us.

That is why we were not really disappointed when the basset walked off and left us without so much as a farewell. We didn't want to become involved simply by doing a good turn for a lost dog.

She left us on a Friday. Saturday was bright and sunny, and the snow in our dooryard began to melt, at last. I went for a long walk, looking for migrant birds, and didn't see one. It was still too wintery, too cold and too much snow, for the robins or even the redwings to arrive. Sunday was sunny too, and we drove past Twin Lakes and down to Lake Wononscopomuc, where we have a small camp. But the ice hadn't even begun to break up on the lakes. It would be another two months, six weeks at least, before I could put my boat in the water. Monday we went to Pittsfield and were caught in snow flurries. Winter just wouldn't let go. Tuesday was warm again, and for the first time since December the ice began to break up on the river. A channel of open water had cleared by early afternoon. The next day was Barbara's birthday, so when I went to the village to have the car greased that morning I bought a toy stuffed dog as a gag present for her. It wasn't a basset, but it did have long, floppy ears and I thought it would give her a laugh. Soon after I got home the florist delivered the bunch of violets she always gets from me, and I decided to add the laughs ahead of time. I gave her the toy dog. She was properly amused, said it was more welcome than its live counterpart because it didn't have to be fed and it never would bark in the night. "This is exactly the kind of dog I wanted."

That afternoon we went for a walk up the road beside the

river and found the first signs of spring—the red osiers were blood red, the riverbank willows were quickening, their withes almost amber in color, and the buds on the shadbush were very fat, getting ready to burst into foamy white blossoms. We walked, and we talked of spring, of bluets and anemones, and of scallions and dandelion greens. We came back down the road, home. And here, sitting on the front steps just as though she belonged here, was the basset. Waiting for us. Expecting us to return and welcome her with open arms. She stood up as we started up the walk, wagged her tail slowly, confidently, watched us with that "Here I am, you lucky people" look again. And Barbara exlaimed, "Well, look who's here!" And then, "She came back for my birthday!"

The dog greeted us with happy but restrained little barks, danced but remembered not to leap at Barbara, and was at the door before we were. She came in ahead of us, romped through the living room and into the kitchen, where she waited expectantly at the refrigerator. Barbara warmed milk, gave her a bowl of corn flakes. While the dog was gulping that down Barbara decided it was meager fare and certainly not in keeping with a birthday, so she opened a can of corned beef hash. That, the dog made it quite clear, was more like living. That was something that would stick to the ribs. She finished the corned beef hash and clearly indicated that she could eat another can of it, maybe two more. But Barbara, the commissary department, decided that one was plenty.

When she had eaten, I put the dog outdoors. She was back within five minutes, ready for more food. She didn't get it and went to the living room, to her chosen place beneath the bench. She made it quite clear that she felt she had come home. We left her there and went to the library and started a game of Scrabble. Within fifteen minutes, here came the dog, obviously wanting to be with people. She looked things over and lay down beside Barbara's chair. Five minutes and Barbara sniffed and asked, "What smells?" I couldn't smell anything special. But she sniffed again and announced, "It's the dog. She gets a bath tomorrow." And she sent the dog back to the living room and closed the door.

Suppertime came and, to my surprise, the dog stayed in the living room. No nosing around the kitchen begging for a snack while Barbara was cooking, and no begging at the table while we ate. I chalked up a couple of good-conduct marks for her.

After supper Barbara phoned Morris, told him the dog had come back and asked what he knew about bassets. Even from where I sat I could hear his laugh. Barbara hung up and said, "He's coming over. He wants to see her."

When Morris arrived the dog looked up at the sound of his car in the driveway. When he slammed the car door she got up and was all attention. When he came up onto the porch she barked, a remarkably deep, thoroughly challenging bark. Morris came in and she was there in the hallway, demanding to know who he was and why he was intruding. He laughed at her and I said, "It's all right. He's a friend," and she calmed down.

"Hey," Morris said, "you've got yourselves a watchdog. As well as a rabbit hound!"

We went into the living room and the dog went to Morris, sniffed. She smelled dog on him, his own foxhound, Lady. He squatted down and rubbed her ears, let her put her forefeet on his knee, inspected her broad chest, her short, stocky legs, her big feet. "Nice dog," he announced. He ran his hand over her sleek skin and felt something in her right flank. I looked and saw that the hair was shorter there, and when he parted the hair there was a scar and the mark of several stitches. She had had a gash several inches long, and somebody had thought enough of her to take her to a vet and have the wound taken care of properly. Morris examined it and said, "I wonder if Dr. Vince did this job. I'm going to find out." He went to the phone and called his neighbor in the village, a veterinarian, but there was no answer. Dr. Vince was out. I said we would call him in the morning, and we went back to the living room and talked dogs for another half hour. Morris agreed that the basset was probably pedigreed, certainly of excellent blood, and was young enough to train as a rabbit dog. "You won't even have to train her," he said. "Just take her up on the mountain and let her go. She'll put up a rabbit and away she'll go. Second nature to a basset."

When Morris left I tried again to reach Dr. Vince, but still there was no answer. Then I tried the veterinarian in Great Barrington, fifteen miles to the north. No answer there either. Evidently it was veterinarians' night out. We called it a day, put the dog out for ten minutes, then bedded her down on the enclosed back porch as before. She was content, and we went upstairs to go to bed ourselves.

"I don't know whether I want another dog or not," Barbara said.

"Nobody asked you," I said. "This one just took it for granted that you wanted her."

"Well, if she stays she's not mine. She'll have to be ours."

"Then you want to keep her?"

26

"I said I don't know. I'll have to think about it." And a moment later she asked, "What would be a good name for her?"

And there it was. She had made her decision. You don't name a dog you don't expect to keep.

I couldn't think of a good name for a basset. Not offhand. And I didn't try very hard that night. Plenty of time tomorrow, I decided.

The next morning I was of two minds about letting the dog out after I gave her a snack of breakfast. I didn't want her to go kiting off before at least greeting Barbara, even if she couldn't really wish her a happy birthday. But I let her out, and she was back within ten minutes, insisted on being let in. It was not a morning that invited casual strolls. The forecast had been for light rain, but up here in the hills it came as snow. More snow, which we certainly didn't need.

The dog came back in, and when Barbara came downstairs a few minutes later and I chanted, "Happy birthday, dear Barbara," the dog seemed to sense celebration. She danced happily, softly barked a greeting and galloped about the library, then into the kitchen ahead of Barbara. And skidded on the linoleum, went sprawling and got to her feet with an absolutely clownish gesture of nonchalance. We laughed at her and she barked again, seeming to enjoy the laughter, even at her own expense. Most dogs act shamefaced or indignant when they are laughed at. Pat resented such laughter. Maybe this dog had a sense of humor, we decided.

Barbara got her coffee, looked out at the falling snow, gave up on the weather. When she was really awake we got breakfast, and about nine she phoned the veterinarian in

Barrington. Yes, Dr. Gulick said, they had had two bassets in
for surgery in the past month. One of them only ten days
ago, so obviously not the dog at our house; but the other
back in February, about the right timing. He gave Barbara
the name and phone number of the owner, a woman in
Monterey, Massachusetts. That seemed a coincidence. The
man who thought Pat might have been his dog had lost his
hound on a mountain in Monterey. Barbara tried to reach the
basset owner in Monterey, got no answer. So she called Dr.
Vince in Canaan, and he said he didn't remember treating
a basset recently, but he would like to see this dog. Were
we coming to Canaan this morning? Barbara said yes, we
probably would, and he said to bring the dog over to his
office, let him look her over.

We had to do some marketing, so we got ready and went
to Canaan in midmorning. Lacking a leash, I took a long
leather thong and tied it to the dog's collar. She thought I
was playing some kind of game, and she wanted to play too.
She grabbed the thong from me and dashed from kitchen
to living room to hall to library. I finally cornered her and
persuaded her to stop romping, took her to the garage, put
her in the car. And we went to Canaan, to Dr. Vince's office.
There she wanted to resume the chase-me game but quieted
down and became interested in all the marvelous dog smells.
Dr. Vince came out and she thought he was a nice man,
went with him to the back room and let him put her on the
examining table. I wondered how she would react, if the
stitches in that flank wound had been painful enough to
make her suspicious. Not a bit of that. She was curious about
what was going on, but that was all. He examined her, said
the wound was well healed, removed the remaining two

stitches, said it looked like a Dr. Gulick job, and we told him what Dr. Gulick had reported. He went on with the examination, said she seemed to be spayed, for her glands were very small, seemed to be inactive. He guessed her age at about three years. Barbara said she wanted the dog to have a bath, to be sweetened up a little, and Dr. Vince said that was easy; just to leave her there while we did the marketing.

So we went down to the market and to the other stores, bought the groceries and household supplies—including an assortment of canned dog food. And I stopped at the hardware store and bought a chain leash and a black leather collar. I wanted no more of this nonsense of chewing a leather thong just for the fun of it. Then we went back to the vet's office. The dog was ready to go, still damp but smelling clean, slightly perfumed. Dr. Vince had even trimmed her nails. She barked happily at us and pranced out to the car. Her car. There were three cars parked there, and she picked the right one the first time. I opened the door and in she went and onto the back seat. And so we came home. It was still snowing, light, slushy snow. Somehow a snow like that in mid-March doesn't seem proper, possibly even illegal.

At home we got old towels and rubbed the dog virtually dry, then let her lie on the rug in front of the hot air register in the front hall. Half an hour there and she came and found me and insisted that she wanted to go outdoors. I put on a jacket and cap and went out with her. She barked at the falling snow and went dashing up the road. I ran after her, calling, ordering, demanding. She ran a hundred yards, turned and came back past me, turned again and was off up the road once more. Games, still playing games with me. I didn't want to play games in that snow. But I followed her a couple of hundred yards. Then she darted off, headed for the woods on the mountainside. I hurried after her, got my shoes full of snow, used all my strongest words and after five minutes decided to let her go. I turned and came back to the house, breathless and angry. And started to tell Barbara what an impossible dog that little bitch was, and how little I cared whether she ever came back. I had barely started my recital when the whining at the front door indicated that she was back. Barbara let her in, told her that she was a very thoughtless dog, chided her for getting all wet and getting her feet and legs and belly muddy, right after having a bath. The dog didn't even bat an eye. She allowed herself to be wiped off again and went to her refuge under the bench in the living room.

We ate lunch, a roast pheasant that we had saved in the freezer for such a special occasion, and when we had finished, right through the angel food cake and ice cream, we played a couple of new records and decided to go for a walk, since it had stopped snowing. So we went, the three of us. This time I put the dog on the new leash, and Barbara tried to hold her in check. It was like trying to check a headstrong ox—she almost pulled Barbara's arm from its socket. How so small a dog managed so much pulling power was a mystery until I began trying to calculate the strength of those stocky legs and the leverage she had in their short length. Finally I took the leash, and she almost dragged me off my feet before I slowed her down. At last she tired of that game and walked at our pace, and when we turned back after half a mile up the road she was content to walk with us, not try to break any speed records.

Home again, we read a while. And Barbara called the

woman in Monterey. That time she got an answer. "We hear," Barbara said, "that you have a basset hound. A female."

"That's right," the woman said. "She is right here beside me this very minute."

Barbara exclaimed, "Oh, thank goodness!" And went on to tell her about the dog we had.

They talked for half an hour, about basset lore, food, habits, temperament, sickness—everything one could imagine. Before they had finished they were on a friendly first-name basis. And when she finally hung up, Barbara said, "Sybil says that bassets are just about the best dogs in the world. Gentle and loving and sturdy and healthy. They do tend to be wanderers, she says, but they come home. Her basset is ten years old and pretty well over the wandering stage. Sybil has four dogs, but her basset is her favorite, apparently. She said to call her any time a problem comes up."

And a few minutes later she asked, "What would be a good name for her?"

So we discussed names, everything from the facetious to the pontifical. Pain-in-the-Neck to Queen Elizabeth. Ariadne to Chloe. Birthday Girl to Iris March. None of them seemed quite right. We took a recess from the naming and I built a fire in the Franklin stove. The dog stood and watched the flames a few minutes, then sat on the rug in front of it, watched the fire intently and lay down, facing it, and went to sleep. And Barbara said, "I wondered, when she took off this noon while you were out, if she would come back."

I said, "She'll always come back now. Just like a bad penny —she'll always come back."

"Penny," Barbara said. "That's it." She called to the dog, drowsing in front of the fire, "Penny. Penny, come here, Penny!"

The dog lifted her head and yawned, looked around at Barbara.

Barbara said again, "Come here, Penny," and the dog got to her feet, stretched and went to Barbara. "There," Barbara said to me. "That's her name, and she already knows it. I wonder what her name really was. Emmy, maybe. Or Jenny. Something with that 'any' sound, I'll bet."

We got supper and ate, and Penny got her evening meal. We sat in front of the fire for a time, talking, and I put Penny outside and she came back and was put to bed on the back porch. Barbara said it had been one of the nicest birthdays she could remember. We sat and watched the embers fade and begin to die, and finally we went upstairs to get ready for bed.

I was half undressed when I heard Johnny arrive. Johnny is the dairy farmer up the road who plows the snow out of our driveway every winter. The snow had stopped in mid-afternoon after giving us another eight inches, but Johnny had his evening milking to do and his barn chores. Then he ate his supper and relaxed a bit, and now he was here to plow out our driveway.

He hadn't much more than started when I heard Penny, all the way downstairs on the back porch. She was growling, the most furious growl you ever heard from a small dog. She barked baritone, but she growled basso profundo. It would scare the living daylights out of a prowler, I thought, for it sounded like the warning of an angry mastiff, maybe a full-grown lion. I listened and I smiled, wondering what she thought was going on outside. Then she began barking, that baritone bark. Threatening, challenging. She barked half a dozen times, waited, barked again. And I, in a robe, went downstairs and tried to make her understand that all was well, that the noise was normal in the circumstances. As long as I stayed there talking to her, she accepted my explanation. The minute I went back upstairs she barked her challenge again.

She barked all the time Johnny was here plowing. When he had finished and gone home she continued to bark. She didn't like the sound of the snowplow; she didn't like the silence, either. And when I went downstairs again to explain the situation to her, she burst past me the moment I opened the door to the porch, raced through the kitchen and library to the front door and stood there barking. There was no way out of it—she had to be taken out and shown. So I went back upstairs, pulled on my pants, came down and put on my storm coat and boots, snapped the new leash on her collar—I wasn't taking a chance on her bolting—and opened the front door. Her lunge out onto the front porch almost took me off my feet. But I held her somewhat in check all across the dooryard and took her to the driveway and garage to show her what all the noise was about. Near the garage she smelled dog—Johnny's dog must have been with him. She sniffed the tracks and wanted to dash right up the road after them. I discouraged that. She marked all three places Johnny's dog had marked. She sniffed the tracks of Johnny's jeep. She inspected the whole apron in front of the garage. And finally I persuaded her to return to the house. We had a bit of an argument at the front steps—she wanted to go back to the garage, probably up the road to Johnny's farmhouse.

But I finally got her indoors, locked the front door, took her to her own bed, removed the leash, got out of my boots and storm coat and went upstairs.

In the bedroom, Barbara said, "Oh, I forgot to tell you. Sibyl said that as soon as Penny settles in she will be a good watchdog."

I laughed, a jeering laugh. "Penny settled *in* several hours ago. Penny already thinks she owns this place. Now all she has to do is settle *down*."

Three ᚙ

It snowed again that night. The snowplows were out before dawn, clearing the roads for the school buses, and Penny woke us up with her barking at them and their noise. But she soon quieted down and was asleep when I got up at five-thirty. She heard me, though, and made it clear that she wanted company, or wanted to be company. I got her a snack of breakfast and let her come into the library with me

35

while I read the papers and had coffee. She indicated that she liked the routine around here.

When Barbara got up I sent Penny into the living room, and Penny went without complaint. Her day had been properly launched. But as soon as the morning warmed up, with a bright March sun, I put an old throw rug out on the front porch and suggested that she go out there. She went, happily, stood and watched the world for maybe five minutes, then lay down and dozed in the sun. She made no move to take off for anywhere, though she was free to go if she had wanted to.

Midmorning and Barbara called our young schoolteacher friend, Emmy Jane, whose school was closed that day. Emmy had heard about Penny and wanted to come over and see her. She came, in her jeep with the snowplow on it. Some folk, and Emmy is one of them, like to be prepared for emergencies. Penny didn't bark once at the jeep or at Emmy. She simply got to her feet and waggled a full-length welcome when Emmy came up the front walk, just as though they had known each other for years. Emmy is a dog-cat-horse person, and I think such people have an aura that most animals are conscious of. I have heard some people say, with a sniff, that it is simply the smell of dogs or horses on them, but I can't accept that. Some of the cruelest men I ever knew, who kicked dogs and beat horses, had on them the smell of dogs and horses that even I could smell. It is something more subtle than a mere odor. In any case, Penny told Emmy Jane that she liked her the first time they met. They came into the house together and within five minutes Emmy was sitting on the floor with Penny in her lap, the two of them talking about the state of their private world.

Before she left, Emmy offered the best theory we had
heard about where Penny came from. "I wouldn't be surprised," she said, "if she belonged to some young couple
from New York who came up this way on a skiing trip. You
see lots of skiers going north every weekend. They could
have stopped in Salisbury or Canaan for lunch and the dog
could have got out of the car or somehow been left behind.
She would be a total stranger here. That could be why nobody seems ever to have seen her before. I'll bet that's what
happened."

We agreed that such an event would answer many of the
questions about Penny. We even tried a few skiing names on
her—Ski Bum, Ski Bunny, Schuss, Slalom, even Boots. None
of them made any impression on her whatever. If she came
from a skiing household she didn't share the conversation.
So her name remained Penny.

When Emmy was gone, having given her blessing, we put
Penny out on the front porch again, and she lay there happily
while we had lunch. Later in the afternoon I went for a
walk with her. Fortunately, I put the leash on her. She
wanted to go down the road, and she didn't want to dawdle
along at my normal three-miles-an-hour pace. So she towed
me, like a tug hauling a barge, at about five miles an hour.
When we had gone half a mile down the road and I stopped
for a breather she sat down and panted quite companion-
ably. When we started back I let her carry the leash—she
liked to mouth the leather loop which served for a handhold. She was content to walk beside me, at my own pace.
But when we got in sight of the house I saw that Johnny
had come down to plow the new snow out of the driveway,
and I took hold of the leash again. Just in time, for she saw

Johnny's jeep a moment later and took off with a lunge that almost took me off my feet. So she towed me the rest of the way home at five miles an hour.

Johnny's dog wasn't with him, which tempered Penny's interest somewhat. Even so, she stood in the road with me, fascinated, and watched the plowing, finally barked, just a token bark. Johnny stopped and shouted, "If she was as big as her bark you could put a saddle on her and ride her. What do you call her?"

"Penny."

"Most underpriced dog I ever saw!" And Johnny went on with the plowing.

We stood and watched till Johnny finished the job and left. Then we came in and Penny settled down for her afternoon nap. There was no more excitement till almost suppertime. Penny was in the living room, under her bench, when a car came past and the driver beeped the horn. It was our friend, Morris, merely signaling that he was passing, as he usually does. He went on without stopping, but Penny barked once from the living room and dashed to the front door. She barked twice more, then whined softly. Not the alarm bark; it was her greeting bark. And the whining was almost affectionate. Evidently she knew it was Morris who drove past and beeped the horn, though I had no idea how she knew. I doubt that she had ever heard that horn, and I know she didn't see the car. It was something beyond my understanding, and still is. She wanted Morris to come back, rub her ears and talk sweet dog-talk again. It was several minutes before she accepted the fact that he wasn't coming back that evening. Then she came into the library to be with us, and we had to be substitutes for Morris.

Another couple of days and it seemed obvious that Penny intended to stay, so we decided we'd better license her and put a tag on her collar. That would both legalize our ownership and give her an identity in case she wandered off or ran away.

I went down to the town hall and told our friend Lila that I wanted a license for a basset hound. "The same one you called me about last week?" she asked.

"Same one."

Lila laughed. "Another dog who came to stay?" And I said no, not another Pat, anyway. Lila reached for her record book, leafed back until she came to the stub for the last license I took out for Pat and showed it to me. Across the top she had written in red ink, "The Dog Who Came to Stay," and across the bottom, "Deceased 12-6-62." "Pat's record," she said, "is going to stay right here, in the archives of the town."

Then she made out a new license, listing the name as Penny; sex, spayed female; owner, Barbara Borland. She gave me the brass tag. I paid the fee and Penny was a legally registered citizen of the Town of Salisbury, County of Litchfield, State of Connecticut. Then I stopped at the local hardware store, which sells almost everything except groceries and baby clothes, and bought a rawhide "bone" and a three-inch rubber ball. I thought the rawhide bone would satisfy her need to chew on things and the ball would be something to romp with and work off excess energy.

When I got home Barbara said Penny had been a problem child. Five minutes after Barbara went to her typewriter, Penny wanted out. Another five minutes and she wanted in again. She wandered about the house. She whined. She cried.

She practically demanded, Where is he? Why did he go away? When is he coming back? Barbara said, "She made me feel like a heel, just as though I had chased you out and wouldn't let you come back."

The minute I came to the door, Penny dashed to meet me. She barked a soft greeting, accepted one pat on her back, then went to her station under the bench in the living room. She lay down and paid me no more attention, even when I went upstairs to my study. It was obvious to me that all she wanted was to know that both members of her household were here. "There isn't any special attachment to me," I said. And I reminded Barbara how restless and uneasy Pat used to be when I was away from the house. But Pat seemed to know when I was merely out on an errand and when I was gone for the day. If I was going to be gone more than an hour or so he was twice as truculent toward outsiders as usual. He was Barbara's guardian and he took his responsibilities very seriously. But if I was at home alone, Barbara away, he seemed to worry. Evidently he didn't think he had to guard me, but he was restless as a cat in a strange house, alert to every sound. He didn't relax and calm down until Barbara returned safely.

"Maybe Penny is going to be a worrier too," I said.

"Pat," Barbara said, "was impossible at times, the way he fussed when you were gone. But he was a great comfort when there was a storm in the air. Remember how he reacted to a thunderstorm?"

I remembered. Pat and Barbara both hated thunderstorms, felt them approaching, were taut as fiddle strings until the storm hit. Then they relaxed. Evidently it was a response to atmospheric pressures. And both of them reacted and were annoyed that I didn't.

"Maybe Penny will have a headache when a thunderstorm is coming," I said. "Maybe you have a summertime pal, too."

I opened the package from the hardware store, called Penny and gave her the rawhide bone. That was a mistake, the first one. I gave it to her right there in the living room. She gnawed it for a minute, then tossed it into the air, watched it bounce off a chair, chased it and sent an end table spinning. She flipped the rawhide bone again, tossed it onto the couch, leaped after it and scattered cushions. Barbara shouted and I grabbed at the plaything, caught it just as Penny grabbed it. We had a bit of a tussle before I convinced her that we weren't playing games. I took the bone back, hid it in my pocket, and for some reason that didn't make a lick of sense ten seconds after I thought of it, I thought the rubber ball would be harmless. I took it out of the package, showed it, then tossed it toward Penny. That was mistake number two, and a lollapalooza. The ball bounced and Penny lunged at it, knocked it aside, raced after it as it rolled. Under a chair, which overturned and fortunately missed the end table with a vase of flowers, past a floor lamp that rocked precariously but didn't quite go over, and under the table with the record player on it.

It wasn't exactly a scene of devastation, but it certainly was an endangered zone. I shouted at Penny, Barbara shouted at both of us, Penny barked and the ball rolled under the sofa. I finally caught Penny by the collar, hauled her away from the sofa where she was trying to dig a hole in the rug to get at the hidden ball. We retreated toward the hallway. Barbara was shooing both of us. "Out! Take her out of here before you wreck the place! Both of you, out!" I got Penny to the front door, opened it, thrust her out onto the porch. And after a moment I went out there too, to let things subside in the house.

Penny was both baffled and indignant. She had been given two fascinating playthings. One had been taken from her, the other had run away and hidden, and she had been banished from the living room. What, she seemed to ask in a rhetorical question to the world at large, what is a dog expected to do with a bone and a ball? Put them in a corner and sit down and watch them do nothing?

Outside, I took the rawhide bone from my pocket and tossed it to her. She nosed it a moment, watching me with a questioning if not actually a suspicious look. Then she flipped it into the air, danced after it, flipped it again. She raced after it with an elephantine thunder of feet. She looked at me. I looked at the door. Barbara didn't appear.

Penny flipped the bone toward the steps, and it bounced down and off the porch. She lunged after it, rolled halfway down the steps, caught herself, grabbed the bone and, in the same sinuous motion, tossed it again. That time it went on down the steps and into the yard. She dug it out of the snow, and the snow seemed to cool off her exuberance a little. She brought it back to the front walk, crouched there and chewed on it for a minute or so, while she caught her breath. Then she picked it up, ran down the walk, crossed the road to the snow-covered riverbank and disappeared. I followed her as far as the road but couldn't see where she had gone. Five minutes later she came back, her muzzle covered with snow crystals. Obviously she had taken the brand new rawhide bone down the riverbank and buried it in the snow. It may be noted here that I never did find that rawhide bone. I have no idea where she hid it, and even she never found it again. She came back to the road, sneezed and rubbed the snow off her muzzle with a forepaw, and came back to the porch with me in an almost sedate state of emotions. She lay down on her throw rug there on the front porch, and I went back indoors.

Before we let her in the house again I retrieved the rubber ball from under the sofa and hid it in the catch-all drawer in the kitchen. She didn't get it again in the house. Two days later I gave it to her out on the porch and it rolled down the steps, was retrieved from a snowdrift, taken across the road and down the riverbank, and it too was hidden somewhere down there. And that was the end of such toys for Penny.

That evening Barbara called her friend in Monterey again. And she and Sybil talked dogs, specifically bassets, for more than half an hour. Never give a basset a ball in the house, Sybil said, unless you want all your lamps broken and your chairs overturned. And Barbara agreed, one hundred percent. A basset will eat almost anything edible, Sybil said. Vegetables are good for them. Her basset specially liked green beans. "Try vegetables on Penny. Actually bassets can digest almost anything. They seem to digest most bones except chicken bones, which should be outlawed for all dogs. Chicken bones are like broken glass, but chop bones seem to present no problem. The basset's jaws are very powerful. A basset simply chews up a chop bone, gets it to an edible place before it swallows it." This, Sybil warned, may violate professional advice, and maybe for some dogs it is all wrong, but that is what she had learned by experience.

43

And she asked, "Does Penny go upstairs?"

Barbara said, "Of course she does. *Gallops* up, in fact."
Sybil couldn't believe it. Her basset simply wouldn't go up a
flight of steps. Down, but not up. And her basset, after ten
years, still had to be chased off chairs now and then. Did
Barbara's Penny? No? Well, that was something? If we ever
had to chase her off, or punish her for anything, a rolled-up
newspaper was the best thing she had found—it made a re-
sounding thwack and it didn't really hurt; it was more of a
surprise and a disgrace than anything else. "Bassets," she
said, "are stubborn as mules. But lovable."

Those last two statements were gospel truth. Especially
the stubbornness.

We had tried various brands of canned dog food, and she
had certain preferences that I wouldn't call acceptance and
rejection—just preferences. But she had refused, absolutely
refused, to eat kibbled dog food, the dry biscuit type of food
that is shaped in what are sometimes called bite-size bits. We
tried it on her plain dry, in milk, in water, soaked to mushy
softness, barely damp, every way we could think of. She
refused to eat more than one mouthful. With a bagful of the
stuff, I began to feed it to the birds. I crushed it to coarse
granules and put it with the grain in the feeders. The birds
ate some, but they kicked a good deal more of it out of the
feeders and onto the ground. And that dog loved it after it
had been put in the bird feeders and kicked out! She would
go out with me to burn the papers or fill the feeders and she
would stand there under the feeders and gluttonize on that
kibbled dog food, some of it still bone dry, some soggy with
moisture. She didn't care what state it was in, she simply

44

gobbled it down. I tried it again in her dish, but she turned up her nose and walked away. Five minutes later she was out under the bird feeders, slurping it up.

But, of all things, she still liked an occasional bowl of cornflakes and milk, and eventually when she was hungry enough, she tried the kibbled food again, out of her bowl, and found that it was almost as good as that under the bird feeders. From time to time she would eat a whole bowl of it. But she always got her ears in the food, especially in anything with milk on it. Those long ears were a problem at mealtime. I suggested pinning them up over her head, like ear flaps on a winter cap, with clothespins. Barbara didn't think that was a good idea. I suggested tying them up with a small scarf. She didn't like that idea either. She called Sybil, who said to get "a long-eared dog dish." I went to the village and found one, a simple arrangement, a rather big bowl with an inner cup to put the food in. The ears didn't drag in it. I bought one and took it home, and Barbara said that Penny hadn't missed me at all. Barbara had played records and Penny had listened with her, lying beside her chair. "She doesn't like *The Music Man,* but she is crazy about Tijuana Brass. Anything with Herb Alpert's trumpet really sends her."

That evening Barbara's friend Anna, who lives over beyond Canaan, phoned. "I hear you've got another dog," she said. "A basset hound."

"Yes," Barbara said, "we've got a dog again. For a while, anyway. Who told you?"

"It was in the paper."

"Which paper?"

"The Waterbury paper."

"Oh. I wonder who put that in?"

Even before they had hung up, I knew who wrote that story. Lila, the town clerk. I told Barbara, and she said, "Well, at least we won't have to advertise her now. More people will read that story than would read a lost-dog notice among the want ads."

Four ⇜

Two days later, after we had done the morning's work at the typewriters, the three of us, Barbara and Penny and I, went for a walk up the road before lunch. It was a beautiful day, brilliant sun and a melting breeze, and high time too, with a foot of snow still on the ground. The road was clean and dry, though, and for the first time Penny didn't try to haul me along like a barge. She walked almost sedately and at approximately our own pace. About a quarter of a mile and Barbara turned back, saying she wanted to get the lunch started and for me and Penny to go on and not hurry back. So we continued up the road another quarter mile or so and seemed to be on terms of complete understanding. Penny was in a rather gently playful mood, something unusual for her. When she played she usually romped and galloped. But now she pranced beside me and reached up to catch the leash in her mouth. I knew what she wanted and finally I humored her—I let her take the leather handhold of the leash, and here she was, actually leading herself. She shook it, made a musical little jingle of the chain. She continued to prance, now with a strut, beside me, matching her pace to mine.

I turned back toward home, and she was willing to do exactly as I did, turn when I did, walk at my pace. She was being Little Miss Perfection with absolutely flawless manners. We walked that way about halfway home and came to the railway embankment, where the stub line of the railroad that once ran from Canaan to Lakeville crosses the river and angles across our farm. The embankment was fifteen feet high and was bordered on both sides by hazel brush, bush dogwood and wild raspberries. A perfect hideout for cottontails, and a place where the red vixen who denned just up the slope often hunted. A place full of odors that were fascinating to a dog's nose. We came to the embankment and Penny stopped, lifted her head, nosed the air. I had a hunch and reached for the leash. But I was an instant too late. Penny leaped from the road into the snow at the foot of the embankment and was plunging into the brush before I was able even to call, "Penny! Come back here!"

I might as well have saved my breath. She didn't hear me. Physically she may have, but emotionally she certainly didn't. She smelled rabbit, or some combination of feral odors that simply couldn't be resisted. Off she went. I followed, into the snow, through the brush, to the cleared roadway at the top of the embankment. I ran after her and caught one glimpse of her, leash dragging, as she dashed through the brush.

I followed her maybe a hundred yards, first calling, then cursing, finally simply puffing. I heard her begin to yelp, in a voice remarkably like Pat's. She had put up a cottontail or hit a warm trail. She was on her way up the mountainside. I stood and listened for a minute or two, both entranced by the sound of her voice and furious at her delinquency. And, even worse, worried about that leash. There it was, dangling behind her, dragging, with that open leather hand loop ready to catch on any stub. Or to slip down between two rocks and jam there. To snag Penny, trap her, make her a prisoner. And a chain, a metal chain, that she couldn't cut with her teeth to get loose. I had visions of her halfway, two thirds of the way up the mountain, snagged by that chain. And me struggling up the snow-clad slopes, wallowing through the brush and the drifts, looking for her. Like as not, the little fool wouldn't bark if she got trapped, wouldn't make a noise that would guide me to her. She would just lie down and wait, quietly. And I would look, and look, and look.

But not now. Now she had gone, was several hundred yards up the slope, in the woods. She would keep going till the rabbit ran in or she got caught, maybe an hour, maybe two miles. I said, "Nuts to you!" and turned and went back down the embankment to the road and went on home.

My shoes were full of snow. My heart was full of resentment.
And, of course, annoyance at myself. I shouldn't have
trusted her with that leash. If I had kept hold of it, this
would never have happened. Angry at myself, I took it out
on her.

I came home, and to Barbara's questions I said, "She ran
away. Went up the railroad embankment, picked up a
rabbit scent and was gone, like that. She'll come back. I
hope."

"I thought you had her on the leash."

"I did."

"What happened?"

"She wanted to carry it, so I, like a fool, let her."

"Oh." There was amusement, a trace of ridicule, just a
tinge of accusation, in that one syllable.

We ate lunch. I went to the kitchen door and listened. No
sound of her up on the mountain. I kept listening, now wish-
ing that she *would* bark, give some indication that she still
was running that rabbit. Not a sound. I turned back into the
kitchen, and Barbara, from the living room, called, "Here
she is!"

I hurried to the front door, thinking she was on the porch.
No Penny. "Where is she?" I asked.

"She was right here in the yard, a minute ago."

I went out onto the porch, called, "Penny! Come here,
Penny!" And turned and saw her going down the road, past
the mailbox, tail high, on a full-fledged spree.

I came back inside for a coat and when I got to the door
again heard her barking, somewhere in the middle pasture.
I ran to the garage, got out the car and gunned it down the

road. I knew I couldn't catch her afoot. She was two thirds
of the way down to Albert's farm when I caught up. She
was loping along, that leash dragging, just as though she
hadn't already run through the snow on the mountainside
the better part of an hour and a half. I honked at her and
she looked back, recognized the car, went to the roadside
and waited, tail still high and waving. I pulled up beside
her, opened the car door, said, "Get in here, you idiot!" And
in she came, onto the front seat, where she sat down like an
honored guest and looked at me, a half-questioning, half-
defiant look. I jerked the leash in, looped it around my arm,
slammed the door and turned around at the nearest barway.
And came back home, giving Penny the silent treatment. Not
one word of recognition.

She knew she was in disgrace. She came into the house—
still on the leash, you may be sure—without a murmur, without complaint, and without one tail-wag. Barbara sensed
my mood and purpose and said nothing to her. I put her on
the back porch and closed the door. We let her sulk for half
an hour, hoping she was thinking about her woefully repre-
hensible conduct. I doubt that she did that, though. What
she had done was as natural to her as breathing.

In any case, when we finally relented and gave her a can
of dog food, she was neither sorry nor chastened. She accepted the dog food as her due, which I suppose it was, and
gulped it like a glutton, which I *know* she was. She bolted it
down, and when she looked at Barbara with that starving
expression of hers, Barbara opened another can for her. She
bolted that one too and indicated she was still hungry. My
turn, so I got her a bowl of Purina bits with milk to see if she

would eat it. Down that went, and still she wasn't satisfied. She got another bowl of bits and milk. I couldn't figure where she put it all, but she indicated that she could eat more yet, so Barbara brought out a lamb chop bone. We had had chops for lunch and Barbara saved the bones, saying, "Sybil said a basset can eat any bones except chicken and fish, so we'll see."

She gave Penny a chop bone, and we stayed to see what happened. I wouldn't have believed it if I hadn't seen it. Penny took that bone, crushed it between her jaws, swallowed, chomped down a time or two, swallowed again, chomped once more with that awesome bone-crushing sound. By then it looked as though she had a sliver caught in the back of her mouth. I risked it—few dogs will allow you to take a bone away, and fewer still will let you reach into their mouths for a bone—I caught her by the lower jaw, forced her mouth open, reached in and pulled out not a sliver but the whole "heel" of that chop bone. She had merely been trying to get it into a better position to crush. She let me have it but wanted it back. I let her have it. She got it into the back of her mouth, came down on it with a crunch that was like the bite of a hundred-ton press in an auto body works. She crushed that heel of a bone, gulped a time or two, swallowed it and asked for more. Barbara gave her another chop bone. When she had crushed and swallowed that one, she went out into the sun on the back steps and lay there for an hour, probably digesting that gargantuan meal.

Two footnotes to that day. Before she was put to bed that night she indicated that she was hungry and got two more bowls of bits and milk. And apparently she slept well. Certainly there were no whimpers or groans loud enough to waken us.

And that day Barbara began calling her Honey. Barbara did. To me she still was Penny. Or any of half a dozen other names not suitable for repetition in the best of company, names that I thought up when she started that rabbit chase up the mountain.

The next day she was a little logy, which was not at all surprising to me. She lay around the house and out on the front porch, and when I went for a walk in midafternoon she went along but without her usual enthusiasm. I really wouldn't have needed the leash, but I wasn't going to have another episode like that of the day before. We walked, she came home looking tired out, and she lay under the bench and grunted for an hour.

By the second day, however, she was her usual ebullient self. That was a Sunday, and I had just returned from the village after picking up the Sunday *New York Times* when the phone rang. Barbara took the call. It was from a young woman who said she understood that we had a stray basset. Barbara asked where she heard that, and the woman said there was a story about it in the Waterbury paper. Barbara said yes, a dog had adopted us, a lost dog. And the woman said she thought our dog might be theirs. Barbara asked about their dog, and the woman said it was a basset, a spayed female just a little over two years old. Evidently she said it was black and tan, because Barbara laughed and said, "Aren't all bassets black and tan?" Then she asked, "Any other identification?"

By then I had got on the upstairs extension so I could hear what was said at both ends. "Well," the woman said, "she may be scarred on her right side. I guess you call it her flank. She got cut a month or so ago and had to be sewed up. By the veterinarian."

That, to me, cinched it. But Barbara asked, "Anything else?"

"She had a red leather collar."

"What was the number of her license tag?" Barbara asked. She was playing for time, or hoping for some impossible loophole. I knew that.

"She didn't have any tag. We kept meaning to get one, but Tom never got to it, and I couldn't, with the baby and all."

Barbara asked where the woman lived, and she told her. Only four miles or so from our farm, in a group of houses on the other side of the river and near the village. Barbara said, "I'll let you talk to my husband," and I took over.

The woman told me substantially the same things, identification marks and all. Finally I said, "The dog we have may be your dog. I think you'd better come over and see. See if she knows you, at least." And I gave her directions, since she didn't know our place.

I hung up and went back downstairs. Barbara was almost in tears. "I guess she's their dog," she said. "The description fits, even to the red collar and the scar on her flank. But why did they have to wait till now? Till Penny got all settled in here, and we got fond of her!"

"The story wasn't in the Waterbury paper till last week."

"They must have known she was gone, for heaven's sake! Why didn't they report her missing, to the dog warden or somebody?"

"They just didn't. After you got off the phone, she said their dog has wandered off from time to time before. Sybil

54

said bassets are wanderers, didn't she? But she always came home. Till this time."

"How long has their dog been gone now?"

"She didn't say."

"Penny was starved when she got here, and she shouldn't have been if she'd been treated right at home. You know that."

"I know. But I'm wondering about the baby."

"Hmmm. Maybe that's the answer. A baby. Penny felt neglected, needed love. Could be, you know."

"No, I can't buy that. When I was a kid every family had dogs and babies, and I don't think either the dogs or the babies felt neglected. But that was before Spock."

"Well, it does explain why Penny looks in every room each time she goes upstairs. She's looking for the baby. Every house has a baby, of course—that's what she would think, wouldn't she?"

A car pulled into our driveway. I went to the door. It was Willis and his wife Bobbie, friends from down the valley. Out to get their Sunday paper and stopping in just to say hello before they went home. Barbara came to the door and we hailed them, invited them in. We needed, Barbara did at least, to talk to someone, and these friends knew about Penny, though they hadn't yet met her.

They came in, loved Penny at sight. And Barbara said, "We just hung up a phone call from someone who says she is their dog."

"Oh, no!" Bobbie exclaimed. "You mean they didn't miss her until now?" Bobbie is softhearted about dogs, though she did say that Penny seemed to be a very small excuse for a dog. She owned a Great Dane for a number of years, one of the biggest and gentlest Danes I ever knew. Daisy was so big she could stand in the middle of a living room and sweep the ash trays off every end table in sight when she wagged her tail, so big that when she got affectionate one day and put her forepaws on my shoulders I had to look up to see her face. Daisy was a super-dog, and when she died of a cancer Bobbie said she never would have another dog. And she has kept the promise. But no wonder she thought Penny wasn't much of an excuse for a dog.

Penny made her own way, however, as she did with everyone. In five minutes Bobbie was down on the floor talking to her. Meanwhile Willis had to hear the whole story, of her arrival, her personality and finally of the phone call. At last he said, "I think we'll stay awhile, if you don't mind. I'd like to see this confrontation. Of the dog, I mean, with these people who think she is theirs. A dog's emotions aren't very obscure. Gran'ing, of course, that a dog has emotions, and I am sure most dogs do. Daisy did. And old Pat did."

Bobbie looked up and laughed. "Penny is just one little *bundle* of emotions. Don't you think so?" she asked me.

"Well, she hasn't much sense, if that's what you mean. Intelligence, yes, but sense, no. . . . Yes, to answer your question, she is an emotional creature. Like so many of you women."

"And," Bobbie said, ignoring the jab, "she probably ran away because of an emotional problem. Daisy wasn't jealous, but if someone came to the house with a child and everybody made a fuss over it, Daisy would go off in a corner and sulk. She never ran away, but there were times when I'm sure she wanted to."

"Well," Barbara said, "you know as well as I do that we don't want another dog. But she adopted us, and she's been here years and years, two weeks at least. It's not so easy just to say good-bye and good riddance."

Penny left Bobbie and went over to her as she was talking. She stood, tail wagging, eyes wide and adoring, waiting for an affectionate word or a friendly pat. Barbara stared at her, frowning. "No, I won't! Go on away. Go lie down."

Penny watched her, baffled.

"Penny!" she said severely. And Penny's ears drooped, her tail sagged and she turned away, the personification of friendless dejection.

"Penny!" Barbara said again, and this time it was a heart cry. She was on her knees, hugging the little dog, hiding her tears.

Five ⟡

Penny looked up when she heard the car pull into our driveway and stop. She barked once but stayed where she was, under the bench. I went to the door. A tall, slim, dark-haired young man and a very thin girl with a small baby in her arms came up the front walk. I stepped out onto the porch, greeted them. His name was Tom. We came into the living room and I introduced them. The girl sat down but Tom remained standing. Barbara asked how old the baby was and the young mother said two months. Tom reached into his coat pocket and handed me a sheaf of papers. I leafed through them—a pedigree and registration, two bills from a strange veterinarian, three color snapshots of Penny.

I glanced at Penny, still there under the bench but head up, looking from one person to another. Willis was watching Penny, and later he said, "She had the most baffled look I ever saw on a dog's face. I could almost hear her saying to herself, 'What do I do now, with *two* sets of people?'" She glanced at me, seemed almost to plead for an answer. But I didn't have the answer.

Tom was saying, "I guess there's no question about who she is, is there?"

"No," I said. "She's your dog."

He shook his head. "She *was* mine, but—well, look. If she won't stay home, if she wants to live here, then she's yours." Then he asked, "What do you call her? We called her Pokey."

Barbara had been listening. Now she said, "Go ahead and call her. See if she comes."

Tom hesitated just a moment, then said, "Pokey, come here."

She got to her feet and wagged, almost embarrassed, and she went to him. He didn't touch her. He just said her name again, "Pokey," with deep warmth and affection. And the dog almost smiled, then went to Tom's wife and stood up, her paws on the girl's knee, and licked the baby's face.

That broke Tom down. He squatted on his heels and patted her and talked to her, and she talked back very softly. Tom began to talk about her. She had all the shots and, yes, she was spayed. A kind of an accident, that was. One of the shots went wrong, he said, and she got an infection in her ovaries, so the vet had to do what amounted to a hysterectomy. The gash on her flank? As near as he could figure, she got that on barbed wire. She really belonged to Tom's wife, Carol. He gave the dog to her as an anniversary gift. But he had done most of the training.

"In training her," I asked, "how did you punish her?"

"Punish her?" He was aghast. "Oh, I didn't ever punish her. I just talked to her till she knew what I wanted, and she did it. . . . Here, Pokey. Here. Right here." And she went to him, lay down where he was pointing his forefinger. He rubbed her ears, fondly. He had proved his point.

"We both worked till a few months ago," he said. "Pokey was at home alone all day. We've got a playroom in the basement and she stayed there. Then Carol got too pregnant to work and she quit, and Pokey was with her all day. But after the baby was born she began wandering. Some days she would come all the way down to the plant where I work, two miles from home, and wait for me at my car. And sometimes she went down to the horse barn—you know, the training track about half a mile from where we live—I guess because something was going on down there, horses and men, activity. She would stay there all day, sometimes. Now and then she even stayed overnight." He shook his head. "And then about two weeks ago she just left and didn't come back. That's when she came over here, I guess."

Carol was talking to Barbara, who had asked what they fed Penny. "We tried just about everything," Carol said. "But she kept getting sick and throwing up. It seemed she couldn't keep anything on her stomach but bread and milk. Sometimes she would eat half a loaf of bread."

And Barbara said that she had eaten almost everything here.

"And didn't throw up?" Carol asked.

"Not once. . . . We've got quite a lot of dog food that you'd just as well take. Canned food, mostly. Oh, she didn't care for kibbled food, the dry stuff, unless we tried it on the birds first!" And Barbara told them about Penny and the bird feeders and the secondhand kibbled bits that she thought were wonderful after the birds had kicked them out of the feeders.

And finally I said to Tom, "Well, she's yours. No doubt about that. I licensed her here in Salisbury, for her own protection. And I put a new collar on her. Keep the collar, but take the tag off and get her licensed in your own town."

Tom hesitated. But for only a long moment. Then he said, "All right, Pokey, you're going home with us." Then to me, "We'll be glad to have her back. But if she doesn't stay, if she runs off again, she's yours."

Barbara had gone to the kitchen with Carol, to get half a dozen cans of dog food. I told Tom which brand we had been using, which she seemed to prefer, and he said they'd never tried that one.

And then they were out on the front porch, all of them, and going down the front walk, Pokey-Penny in the lead, just as though she was leading an Easter parade. She went down the walk and turned up the road, as though she were going for a walk. She had got past the garage when Tom called to her. "Pokey! Come on, Pokey. Get in the car. We're

61

going home." And she turned back, hesitated an instant, then hurried to the car and climbed in while Tom held the door open. Carol got in, with the baby, and Tom started the motor. He backed out and turned down the road, and a moment later they were gone.

We came back in, and Willis and Bobbie said they wouldn't have missed it for anything. "The look on that dog's face," Willis said, "when they came in, was unbelievable. It was almost as though she was seeing ghosts. And then she was torn between you."

We discussed the meeting and the departure a few minutes, and they left. And Barbara said, "Well, she is gone. It was a happy experience. I'm glad we had her. And I'm glad she is gone, since she really did belong to them. There wasn't any doubt about that, was there?"

"None in the world."

We got lunch and ate. I showed Barbara the clipping from the Waterbury paper that was headed, "Another Dog Who Came to Stay at the Borlands?" It told about the basset hound that had adopted us, and it told the bare outline of the Pat story.

Barbara laughed. "So that's why Lila wanted all the details."

"It's a good story, and she handled it just right."

After lunch we went for a ride in the car, down to our lake place fifteen minutes from the farm. But there still was too much snow in the driveway to get beyond the entrance. We went on foot to the brow of the hill and looked down and saw that the lake was still iced in. It would be the end of May or early June before Barbara could swim. We came home, telling ourselves that we were lucky, at that. No dog to tie us down, to worry about if we went away for the day.

We came home and I got a carton and we put all the rest of the dog food in it, and the dog dish, the dog brush and the leash. I took them down cellar. Barbara handed me the old Navy blanket. "Hang it on the line. Let it air a few days before we even send it to the cleaner."

All right, so she might be back on our doorstep tomorrow morning. Well, not tomorrow, because they would certainly keep close watch the first few days. But within a week she might be back. We weren't betting either way, but we were saying we were glad we had known that particular dog, and now we were saying good-bye, farewell and that's that. It was a pleasant story, and now it had a happy ending.

The next day I got up and automatically started to the porch door to say good morning to Penny. Opened the door, looked, shook my head and went back to the library with my first cup of coffee. Habit is hard to break. But that day I did succeed in breaking the logjam in a book I was writing. The chapter that had been stubbornly impossible to write fell into line at last, and I had that one licked. And Barbara was at her desk, at work. At lunch we agreed that we missed Penny—"No use lying about it"—but it was better this way. And when we went for a long walk that afternoon we saw that the ice on the river was almost all broken up. At long last. We saw two mergansers, the first of the season.

Then it was the day of the vernal equinox. It should have at least looked a bit like spring. But there was still a foot of snow on the ground and before the day was out it snowed again, another six inches. It seemed ridiculous to have to plow snow on the twenty-first of March. Some years we had been out plowing ground on the day of the equinox, though

I admit there was frost in the ground and Albert didn't plow more than a couple of acres that day.

Another week and I phoned Tom, asked him to take the license tag off the dog and mail it to me. I told him I had canceled it at the clerk's office and that he had better license her in his own name. He said he would get to it. He had been busy. But Pokey, he said, was staying at home "pretty good. She was gone all one night, and we thought she had gone back to your place. But she was home next morning and has been home ever since." I asked if she was eating, and he said yes, she ate a good deal.

"Does she still get sick and throw up?"

No, he said. "She hasn't been sick once since we brought her home. I guess it was all that bread she was getting."

But he didn't mail me the tag. It didn't come, and I didn't press him.

Slowly the season progressed. The snow melted in the pastures. By the end of the month the migrant robins were back and the willows were on the verge of bursting bud. And then, the last day of the month, a phone call came and Barbara took it, and a voice strange to her said, "Mrs. Borland, your dog is here." I heard her exclaim, "What!" and then she asked me to take the phone. It was a man I had known several years before when he was a butcher, and now he was working for the lime company about five miles from here. "Your dog is here," he said to me. "The basset hound. She's got a tag, and I traced the number at the town clerk's office."

I said, "Keep her there, Bob. Tie her up or something. We'll be right over."

We got in the car and started to the lime company's plant,

debating what to do, to bring the dog home or take her back to Carol and Tom. We still hadn't decided when we got to the office. I parked in the white-dusted driveway and went into the white-dusty little office building with windows covered with fine white limedust. My friend Bob was at a desk, and the moment I walked in here came Penny, herself looking pale and grizzled with the all-pervading lime. But it was Penny, all right. Penny-Pokey. I thanked Bob, who said she simply wandered in a couple of hours before, made herself at home and got acquainted with everybody. He saw the tag on her collar, made the phone call to Lila and then called our house. I thanked him again and opened the door. Penny went out ahead of me, jaunty and self-confident, went right to the car, waited to be let in. Barbara greeted her coldly, made her ride in the back seat and wouldn't even pat her once. But she said to me, "Let's take her home first. She looks starved."

So we went home, and the moment Penny was let out of the car she went up the front walk and waited at the door for us. Inside, she went through the living room and to the kitchen, stopped at the refrigerator and plainly indicated that she was ready to eat. I went downstairs and brought back a handful of puppy biscuits. She would have nothing to do with regular dog biscuits, but those half-size puppy biscuits were like candy to her. We fed her half a dozen of them, and Barbara said, "We'd better take her back. Anyway, I want to see where they keep her."

So I called and Carol answered. She didn't even know that Pokey-Penny was gone. She had been there the last time Carol looked. Which must have been around noon, since she had been at the lime plant a couple of hours and it was three o'clock when we got her. Yes, Carol said, of course they would like to have her back. Should she come and get her? No, I said, we would bring her. If Carol would give me directions to find the house.

It was a neat, relatively new house with a big lot, at least half an acre, on a gentle hillside in a cluster of maybe a dozen houses on similar lots. Six or eight children, none of them as much as ten years old, were playing nearby. There were two dogs in sight, both small tan mongrels. Children and dogs both watched as we pulled into the driveway. Inside the two-car garage was a conventional doghouse, and a long chain with a snap on the end was fastened to the corner of the garage.

We drew up and Carol came to the door facing the garage. We got out, and Penny looked at Carol, seemed to duck her head and look away, then went in the open door. Carol looked down at her as she passed and said, "Pokey, aren't you ashamed?" Then looked up at us, smiled, asked us in.

We went through a clean, neat kitchen to a conventional living room with its sofa and two side chairs, its television set and coffee table. Penny-Pokey had taken her place in the corner back of the big upholstered armchair, her special corner, we learned. The baby was asleep in the other armchair, still small enough to lie flat in it.

We had just sat down when a car drew into the driveway and Carol said, "It's Tom. He gets off at four on Wednesdays."

A moment later Tom came in the back door, saw us and said, "I wondered if it wasn't you." Then he saw Pokey-Penny in her corner, said, "What did you do, Pokey? Run away again?" She came out to him, all apology and appeal, and he rubbed her ears, talking softly to her. Meanwhile the baby woke up, cried for attention, and Carol went and picked her up, brought her back to where Tom was still communing with Pokey-Penny. "Oh, hello," Tom said, turning to the baby. "How has she been today?"

"A little fretful." To us Carol said, "She's cutting teeth."

Tom turned to Pokey-Penny again. "Go lie down now." She went back of the chair and he shook his head. "I don't know what to do with her. She just won't stay home if I'm not here. Weekends she's with me, won't leave me. But I guess she gets lonely. And Carol's busy with the baby, so she wanders off. Why don't you take her and keep her?"

But Barbara said no. Then she asked Carol, "You like her, don't you? And she's good around the baby?"

"I love her!" Carol exclaimed, and she obviously meant it. Pokey-Penny wasn't being mistreated. She had a good home.

Tom was saying, "But if she won't stay here, if she keeps running off, going over to your place—"

"She didn't come to our place today," I said, and I told him about the phone call from the lime plant, how we went down there and got her.

"Oh. Clear down there. She never went down there before."

I said, "I canceled her license in Salisbury, so I think we'd better take the Salisbury tag off."

"Yeah," Tom said. "Yeah. I've been meaning to get her a license over here, but—well, you know, you put things off." He got a pair of pliers and took the tag off Penny's collar and handed it to me. "Tomorrow. I'll try to get the license tomorrow. If you're sure you don't want her now."

"No," I said. "She's yours, and your wife says she loves

her, and you obviously do." I laughed. "She's your problem child."

"That's for sure," Tom said, shaking his head.

We started to the door.

Carol, the baby in her arms, said it was good to have seen us and she thanked us for bringing Pokey home, was sorry we'd been put to that trouble.

Tom said, "Yeah, much obliged. I hope it won't happen again."

The two of them were at the door as we left. Penny nowhere in sight. The youngsters were still playing Indian, or whatever called for all that war whooping, on the vacant lot down at the corner, and the two tan mongrels were playing coyote. I drove back to the main road and we came home.

Six 〜

The chilly weather persisted. Flickers didn't come back till the first week in April. Daffodils came up but didn't show buds till mid-April. And we didn't hear the spring peepers till April 14, a good two weeks later than usual. By then we were so hungry for spring that when I came home and told Barbara I had heard them she said, "Come on! I want to hear them too!" So we drove to the little bog a mile up the road and sat and listened to the peepers and the redwing blackbirds for half an hour. It sounded like spring, at last. When we got home the temperature was 62. But it dropped into the 20s that night.

The next day was opening day for trout fishing. Morris stopped in that evening. He is a fisherman, one of the best, but he seldom goes out on opening day. He waits till the first-day folk have come and gone, then goes to his favorite holes up the brooks and comes back with his limit. We talked fishing and weather and wondered why it seems always to rain or sleet or snow on opening day. We decided it was a plot but couldn't decide who to pin it on. But we didn't really care.

Finally Morris asked, "Where's the basset?"

We told him, and he said, "I'll bet you miss her. She was a nice little dog."

"We miss her," Barbara said, "like a headache!"

Morris laughed at her, remembering how she felt about Pat and how she treats his dogs when he brings them over. She practically cried when Lady, his gallant old foxhound, was lost on the mountain most of one afternoon, and she took her in, fed her, comforted and cozied her when she finally came limping down here to the house. She even likes Smoke, the big black Newfoundland that comes with him occasionally. Morris is the only man I ever knew who hunts with a Newfoundland. Incredible, but he hunts partridges with Smoke. She has a good nose, she stays close by, she puts up birds without pointing and she is a pretty good retriever. They have a lot of fun, up on the mountain in bird season.

Morris laughed at Barbara, but I knew what she meant.

She didn't want to miss Penny, who aggravated her and annoyed her and was an insinuating nuisance. Yet she couldn't deny Penny's winning ways. To her, Penny was a delight and an absolute exasperation. Yes, she missed her— like a headache, as she said.

I said, "Good riddance," and I switched the conversation to foxes. Morris loves to run them with his hound and listen. I don't think he has shot a fox since I have known him, close to twenty years, but he keep a foxhound and he knows more about foxes than anyone else I know. Get him on foxes and he will talk for an hour.

We had a fine fox evening.

Three days later Barbara and I had to go down to New London for a meeting and a speech, and we were thankful all the way that we hadn't had to take Penny to a kennel and remember her woeful complaints. Pat always seemed to think he was being abandoned when we left him at a kennel. He was being abandoned and we were going somewhere that would be exciting and full of wonderful scents and ripe bones and other dogs. And he made us feel like heels for going. Then we had the chore of apologizing when we got home, after we had gone and got him from the kennel and taken him home and assured him that we still preferred him to any other dog in the whole world.

We went to New London with a clear conscience and no dog complaint ringing in our ears, and we saw friends the next day, and we took our time about coming home.

Home, we found three daffodils in bloom on the riverbank. It was April 22. And two days later it snowed again, a couple of inches of snow that turned to rain and washed away. But it had been snow, and I resent snow after mid-April, I bitterly resent it.

In spite of the snow, there were mallards on the river and poking along the brushy banks, obviously looking for nesting places. And the next morning there were two deer in the home pasture, just back of the woodshed. They were very tame, or very hungry for grass, or both. But when a car came along the road they didn't linger. They were at the far fence in a dozen long bounds, and up and over and out of sight in the brush at the foot of the mountain. They were does heavy with fawn.

Then it was April 28 and a brown thrasher was loudly ecstatic in the tallest apple tree in the back yard. Maybe that was what turned the trick, that brown thrasher. He summoned change. On May Day the temperature got up to 74, the box elders showed first leaf tips and the sugar maples in front of the house began to leaf out. We went down to the lake place and found columbines in fat bud and tall meadow rue shooting up like weeds. It seemed strange to see so many hepaticas still in bloom that late, but they made the glades beside the lake lavender with their color. No swimming, though. The lake's water was only up to 56, and there was a gusty wind that whipped the water into frothy rollers that practically boomed against the rocky shore.

The next few days signaled spring, at last. Bloodroot was in bloom, and early saxifrage, and a few violets. The big popple just up the road was in catkin, long, dark reddish-brown catkins big around as a lead pencil. And then, on May 6, it snowed again, on a day when the peepers were particularly loud. Only about an inch, and it was gone by evening, but snow just the same and an insult to spring. I decided to have nothing more to say about the weather in my journal until the Fourth of July.

Two days later Penny arrived again.

I had gone to the village to mail some urgent letters, and when I came home I saw two dogs coming down the road. One looked familiar. Sure enough, it was Penny-Pokey, looking sleek and self-satisfied and thoroughly independent. With her was a nondescript white mongrel, one of those skittish dogs that are constantly on the dodge, expecting a kick or a thrown stone. They came past the garage just as I stopped at the mailbox, and Penny hesitated, looked at me, wagged her tail, obviously wanted to be greeted and welcomed. I ignored her, took the mail on into the house, then went back to put the car away. The dogs had vanished, absolutely vanished as though they had disappeared into thin air.

I decided not to tell Barbara that Penny had been here. We went through the mail. One letter required an immediate answer, a business matter, so I went to the upstairs telephone and called New York. While I was talking I heard Barbara at the front door, then heard her shout, "Here is Pokey-Penny!" I heard her open the door, heard the rattle of claws on the bare floor of the hallway.

I finished my call and went downstairs.

"Look who's here," Barbara said, half triumphant, half annoyed. "I heard her whining on the porch and went to the door, and there she was."

"Where's the white mongrel?"

"What white mongrel?"

"I saw the two of them, coming down the road together, when I came in the driveway."

Barbara shook her head. "She was all alone when I went to the door."

I went out onto the porch and around the house. No sign of that white dog. I came back in and Barbara had gone to the basement and got the dog food, put out a dish for Penny. She gulped down three handfuls, wagged her thank you and went happily into the living room and flopped in her favorite spot, beneath the bench.

"Well?" Barbara looked at me.

"What do you want to do now?"

"Send her home, I guess. But it's like—well, adopting a child and then sending it back to the orphanage."

"Oh, not exactly like that. She—"

Barbara turned and went to the phone. She called Carol. "Penny's here," she said. There was a pause. Carol was talking. Then Barbara said, "I think you'd better come and get her," and she hung up.

"She says"—Barbara turned to me—"Penny wouldn't eat her breakfast. They put her outdoors and ten minutes later she was gone. She thought Penny was over here, but she kept thinking she would come home." She sighed. "She'll be over."

Fifteen minutes later Carol arrived. "I just don't know what to do if she keeps on like this," she said. "We'll have to do something."

"Let us know," Barbara said, "if you have to get rid of her. Meanwhile, if she shows up here we'll feed her and treat her kindly and either take her home or call you to come and get her."

"I guess that's all we can do. But I do hate to impose on you." She left, Pokey-Penny with her, rather shamefaced and sullenly obedient.

Barbara turned to me. "What else could I do? What else could I have said?"

"Nothing. You said the only thing there was to say."

Hindsight is easy, I know, and practically infallible. But I still say I knew then that the Pokey-Penny problem wasn't solved. She was going to be in our lives awhile longer, no matter what we did or said. But for then it was settled and life could go on without her disruptions or distractions.

The pear tree beside the garden came to dazzling white bloom, ten days ahead of the apple trees. The asparagus finally came up, blue with the cold. Nights persisted chilly, the temperature down in the 30s. We went hopefully down to the lake and found the water there was only 57 degrees. Barbara will swim in water so cold it gives me chilblains just watching her, and she thought, on May 18, with a bright sun and a breeze that had no obvious icicles on it, that she would take her first swim. She got into her suit and I, still fully clothed and wearing a heavy sweater, went down to the dock with her. She sat on the dock and dangled her feet in the water until they turned blue as the dungarees I was wearing.

"It's really not very cold," she said, gripping one hand tightly with the other and practically hunching her shoulders up to her chin. "But," she said, "I don't think I'll go in today. I've changed my mind."

"Darling," I said, "you have occasional flashes of incredible wisdom. Why don't we go back to the farm and heat up the pea soup and sit in front of the fire and eat soup. There's always another day."

And, amazingly, that is exactly what we did.

But on May 27, two weeks late, at least, we had shirt-sleeve weather, the lake temperature got up to 60, and Barbara went for her swim. She didn't swim far, but she went in and swam out and back, and lay in the sun afterward and thawed out and said she was a very brave girl. I said she was not only brave but foolhardy and suggested that she take both antihistamines and antibiotics when we got home. She called me a sissy, which I am, of course. Water colder than 80 degrees is unfit for human occupation, in my estimation, unless one is safely inside a boat that doesn't leak and cannot be capsized.

Then we had a summery weekend, really summery, with the air temperature up to 85 and the water temperature all the way up to 70. Morris helped me take the boat down to the lake and launch it, and I went for my first sail of the season. Barbara swam. It was a beautiful weekend.

And here at the farm summer had arrived. Lilacs were in full bloom, so fragrant we could smell them inside the house, apple blossoms were just past their prime and the petals had begun to fall on the grass like the snow we had had only two or three weeks earlier. The brooksides were purple with violets and the old meadow down the road where it hasn't been mowed for three years was covered with bluets.

That was Memorial Day weekend, and we spent two whole days at the lake, coming home to sleep only because the beds here are more comfortable than the built-in bunks at the boathouse. And both evenings when we came home at dusk Barbara stopped and looked at the front porch before she went up the walk.

The second evening I asked, "What's the matter? What are you looking for?"

"Nothing," she said, and we came on into the house. But a few minutes later she said, "I have a feeling that she will be back."

"Oh?"

"I didn't want to say anything, but—"

"Look, Cassandra, put away the crystal ball. Ask me. I have known since—oh, ever since the first day she came here —that she will be back. The Bad Penny. There's no escaping it. *But she ain't back yet!* . . . Forget it, kid, till she yips at the door."

"I still have the feeling—" She sighed.

There was work to be done in the woods down at the lake, and George had promised to get at it as soon as he finished another job. George is a professional forester and one of the best men in the woods that I know. I phoned him, and he said, "I tried to reach you an hour ago."

"When can you come?"

"Tomorrow morning."

"Meet you there, pal. What time do you get going?"

"How about eight o'clock?"

"As you say. Eight A.M. tomorrow."

The next morning I was at the top of the hill at the lake place thirty seconds ahead of George. He had his truck with chain saw, hand saw, axes, ropes, gear. His man would be along, he said. We drove down to the boathouse and George and I began ranging the property, George marking trees that needed to be taken out with a squirted X from a spray can of yellow paint.

"We'll burn the brush in the driveway," George said.

His man arrived and set to work on the marked trees. George and I finished the lower hillside, and I said I'd like a couple of cords of firewood saved. Then I came home, knowing the job would be done right. George would save every good seedling and sapling possible, and he would cherish every clump of ground hemlock, as we call it. He would know the yellow lady's slipper plants and protect them. He would take as good care of that hillside as I would, maybe even better.

I came home, and I was barely in the door when Barbara said, "We've got a dog."

"What? Again?"

"For good this time. Carol phoned about an hour ago, said they have to get rid of her and would we please take her. I said yes."

"Of course."

"I said you were down at the lake and we would be over and get her as soon as you got home."

"All right, put on a jacket and come on."

She hesitated. "Are you sure?"

"Aren't you?"

"I think so. I know we have to take her now. Something's happened. She's been snapping at the youngsters over there."

"Ohhh. Teasing her, I'll bet."

"That's all she said, that Penny-Pokey has turned vicious.

She snapped at the kids and almost bit a little girl, their next-door neighbor."

She had her jacket. I went to the garage for the car. Barbara got in, and I went back to the house, found the leash. Then we went to get our dog.

Seven ⚬~⚬

She was lying in the driveway, tethered by the long chain and as far from the house and garage as she could get. When we turned into the drive she looked up but didn't move. I stopped the car, got out, and she gave me a "What are you doing here?" look. It was almost an "I hate the world" look, too. Then I noticed that several children were standing across the yard, watching silently.

Barbara came around the car and said, "Penny!" and Penny looked at her, a kind of "So what?" look. Then she got to her feet and went back toward the garage, dragging the chain, which jingled softly on the concrete.

Tom came to the door, invited us in. Barbara said, "No thanks. We haven't much time." Carol came and repeated the invitation, got the same answer. Tom went back into the house. Carol said the same things that had been said over the phone, about her turning snappish, almost biting one of the neighboring youngsters.

"I don't know what's got into her, I really don't. But Tom finally said we'd just have to get rid of her. So—"

Tom came back and handed me an envelope. "The papers. Everything is there, I think." He shook his head, started to say something, then stopped. "At least, there aren't a lot of kids over at your place for her to snap at." Then he added, "But she never snapped at us. Never."

I got the leash from the car, unsnapped the chain from her collar, fastened the leash. She got to her feet, almost resignedly, and went to the car with me. I opened the door and she got in, settled herself on the back seat. Barbara said good-bye to Carol, I shook hands with Tom, and he said, "If you can't do anything with her—well, do whatever you think best. She's yours now."

The neighbor youngsters were still watching, now wide-eyed and grinning, as we backed out of the driveway and started home. Penny sat up and stared out the window, but she didn't look back. She looked sad, almost surly, and she was very thin.

Barbara said, "Carol told me she hasn't been eating.

Didn't want the dog food and wouldn't eat bread and milk any more."

We got home, and the minute she got out of the car she headed for the front porch, dragging the leash. I put the car away. Barbara let her in and when I got to the house Penny was on the back porch eating kibbled dog food moistened with milk. Eating like a starved child. She cleaned up one dishful and we gave her another. She put that away and started on a third before she was satisfied. Then she went in and lay down in her favorite place, under the bench.

She slept for an hour, then went to the front door and wanted out. I let her out. She went down the walk and took off up the road. I thought she would soon be back, but half an hour passed and no Penny. We got out the car and drove a mile up the road, watching and listening. No sight or sound of her. We went down the road a mile and a half to the little bogland where we always hear the peepers first, and still no Penny. "Well," I said, "that's that. Nice knowing her. I hope she enjoyed that meal."

"I hope," Barbara said, "that she has a great big tummy ache! She's an ungrateful little brat!"

"Tut! I'm the one who calls her names." And we managed to laugh. "Maybe she just has to prove her independence," I said. "She has been badgered and scolded, and she has been chained up. And probably teased by those neighborhood kids. She got snappish and stubborn as a mule. So now she has to run away from us, just to prove that she can do what she wants to. . . . How's that for animal psychology?"

"Oh, very good indeed. Where did you learn so much about canine reactions?"

"Studying my own, of course."

Barbara laughed. "You can supply the obvious reply to *that!*"

We were almost back home. I thought I heard something, so I stopped the car and turned off the motor to listen. Sure enough, up on the hillside beyond the home pasture a dog was barking. Penny. Barking "treed," which with Penny would mean she had something cornered on the ground. I hoped it wasn't a porcupine. Or a skunk.

I started the motor and drove on home, got the .22 rifle and struck out across the pasture and up the hillside. Sure enough, Penny had cornered a young woodchuck. Evidently she saw me coming and mustered the courage to close in just before I got there. She had made her final rush, with a flurry of yips and growls and squeals and a snapping of teeth, just as I rounded the last clump of bushes. There she was, shaking the dead woodchuck.

I praised her, thinking maybe we had another Pat—he was a famous woodchuck hunter. She wagged her tail at the praise but didn't trust me. She carried her kill down to the edge of the pasture, rolled on it, grabbed it and hauled it away when I tried to take it from her. But after two more rolls she let me put the leash on her and went home with me without any fuss, though she did want to go back to the dead 'chuck a couple of times. A huntress, that's what she was, by blood and inheritance. And she'd had no chance to get it out of her system.

She was in the house only half an hour when she wanted out again. We let her go, remembering that she had to assert her independence That time she went down on the riverbank and found a fine place to wade, a very special place. She came back ten minutes later smeared with sticky black river muck. So I got a pail of water and gave her a bath. She didn't appreciate the bath, wouldn't even let me dry her off with an old towel. She rolled in the grass and dried herself to her own satisfaction. Then she lay on the front steps for a time.

I didn't miss her until I heard her up on the mountainside again about five-thirty. This time it was her trail bark, not the "treed" or "cornered" bark. She barked from time to time for an hour or so, then was silent. I made no move to go and get her, decided that she would come back when she felt like it or not come back at all. Or maybe stay out all night and come home in time for breakfast. She was silent for a long half hour, then barked the trail bark again. Apparently she had put up another rabbit. Then silence once more. And finally, about a quarter to eight, she came back, tired and filthy again—evidently she had found and wallowed in every seep spring and mudhole on the whole mountainside. I wiped her off and brushed her a bit, and we let her in, fed her two more dishfuls of dog food. Then she lay down under her bench and slept the sleep of the utterly weary. About eight-thirty I took her out to Pat's old place, the little brooder house, and put her to bed on a fresh pallet of straw. It was obvious that she didn't appreciate it. I don't know what she wanted, maybe wall-to-wall shag rug, with a special pad for a mattress. Anyway, she let me know, even before I closed and latched the door, that she didn't think this was much of a place to quarter a dog of her standing. I didn't agree. I came back to the house. And I was barely inside when she began to bark, an impatient bark, then an imperious bark, then a defiant bark and finally a most piteous bark. Barbara looked at me, and I looked at her, and we both shook our heads. And about nine o'clock Penny settled down and shut up.

We were sleeping soundly when a car woke me up about half past twelve. Some idiot came up the road with his car radio on full blast. It was bad enough to wake people, but it was inexcusable to wake sleeping dogs. Penny came to with a roar of indignation and warning. It sounded as though she would tear down walls to get at this intruder. Not only tear down walls but stop the car and haul the driver out and dismember him, maybe disembowel him. I never heard a more peremptory challenge. It was a performance that would make lions quail.

But by then even the echo of the radio-loud car had died, and soon Penny's performance subsided to ordinary barking. That eased to spasmodic barking, the spasms just far enough apart that one could almost doze off between them. Almost, but not quite. This went on for twenty minutes, by the clock —it seemed two hours—and I was tempted several times to get up and go out and tell her to stop it before she got a case of hiccups or something. But each time, she shut up before I even got out of bed, and finally she stopped altogether. I lay awake another half hour, waiting for the next spasm, and finally drifted off to sleep. And we slept the rest of the night.

Apparently she got most of the "I won't" out of her that one day. She was her familiar friendly self when I went to let her out. She frolicked ahead of me to the house, ate a big bowl of breakfast, went outside for ten minutes and came back and asked to be let in. She was the perfect house dog. I had to go to the village in midmorning to do several errands, and Barbara said Penny wouldn't let her out of her sight while I was gone, as though Barbara was her special responsibility.

That afternoon she napped in the house for an hour, went for a long walk with us, then lay on the front steps till about five o'clock. Then she went out across the pasture and prowled the mountainside, barking trail from time to time, for almost an hour. When she came back she hadn't wallowed in one seep spring, hadn't been down in the river mud and wasn't in a nasty mood. She came back, asked to be let in, ate her evening meal, napped in the living room till nine o'clock. Then she went off to bed in the brooder house without a whimper. And she slept all night, apparently. At least she didn't rouse us with any tantrums.

The next morning Barbara said, "Penny seems to have got hold of herself. I think she's going to settle down all right."

Two days later we took her down to the place at the lake.

It was a beautiful June day, sunny and warm and with just enough air in motion to be comfortable. The camp there is a cabin with a living room, a tiny kitchen and two small dressing rooms. It has a six-foot deck across the front facing the water. The lakeshore there is precipitous, with a drop of about twenty feet from the deck to the water's edge. A series of steps go down over the ledge to the dock. There is a ten-foot overhead glass door opening onto the deck, so one gets the feeling of being right outdoors and, on the deck, suspended in midair.

Penny left the farmhouse merely pleased at going for a ride. She loved to ride in the car. She slobbered on the window and slithered on the seat, smirked at the big black cat down the road and looked superciliously at the police dog just beyond. Then she lay down and dozed for ten minutes. She woke and sat up when we got to the top of the hill at the lake place. This was something new, a new woodland and, undoubtedly, brand new smells. She sniffed, at any rate, and watched with intense interest as I drove down the steep, winding road to the parking place just above our camp. When we got out she turned and looked at the lake, probably more water than she had ever seen. She stared at it, trembling. Then she went down the steps to the cabin with us, went in, looked around. At the two built-in bunks, at the chairs, at the two chaises. Then at us, with a "What's this all about?" look.

I opened the big front door to the deck. Penny watched, then hurried to see what was outside. A deck. A platform with narrow spaces between the floor boards, with a railing across the front. She went to the railing, took one look, almost sat back on her haunches. Then she edged forward again, looked at the tops of the gray birches, the shadbush, the mountain honeysuckle that grew beneath the deck, looked down at the dock with the sailboat lying on it, bottom side up, looked out across the water toward the far shore, almost a mile away. Then she looked up at Barbara, standing beside her at the railing, and wagged her tail tentatively. She looked at me. Obviously it was all right or I wouldn't let Barbara stand there at the rail. Penny looked again, then turned and went inside and lay down in the sun. It was quite clear that she could take the camp and the lake or leave them, that she was not a spaniel or any other breed that loved the water. I was sure she could swim—any dog can swim, apparently—but I was equally sure that she would never go swimming just for the fun of it.

Barbara changed to a suit and went down to the dock. I

put on trunks and followed her. She swam. I got in the kayak and went out with her quite a way. Barbara is a fish, or an otter. The water is her element. I can swim, but I would rather not. A dry-land plainsman by birth and up-bringing, I don't trust water without a boat under me, and not all the way even then. I enjoy sailing a small boat or paddling a kayak, but swimming is a chore for me. So I accompanied her in the kayak, and after her swim, while she lay in the sun and basked, I took the sailboat out for half an hour.

Coming back in, I heard Penny barking excitedly at the cabin. Barbara was still down on the dock. She called to Penny, tried to quiet her, but she seemed to be excited by the sailboat, that big expanse of white sail, maybe. She danced all over the deck, barking. I docked the boat. Barbara had gone up to the cabin. Penny was quiet. I heard Barbara say, "Penny, Penny, Penny," gently scolding. I took in the sail and went up the steps to the cabin. Barbara had a rag and was mopping up a corner of the linoleumed floor. Penny sat across the room from her, crestfallen.

"What happened?" I asked.

Barbara shook her head. "She got so excited, apparently over the sight of the boat coming in, that she spilled. Just as I came in the door. She knew what she had done. She must have been trained not to wet the floor. She seemed to expect to be walloped, maybe with a rolled-up newspaper."

We got the floor dried, and I put away the sail and hauled in the boat, flipped it over on the dock—I don't like to bail a boat, so I haul mine and turn it over on the dock, and let it drain. We dressed, closed the cabin and went up to the car. Penny was so glad to get away from the cabin and that frightening deck that she didn't even use the steps; she went right up the slope, through a clump of ground hemlock, over a stump and around a big boulder. She was the first one in the car.

We got home, and Penny didn't even wait to come into the house. She got a drink at the cow trough, then went across the home pasture and up the mountainside. It was just before five o'clock. She was gone till almost eight, when she came home sopping, bedraggled and bushed. Whether it was a reaction to the trip to the lake or what it was, I had no idea. But she had to go, and she had to stay. And she had to come back looking as though she had spent half her life in a mudhole. She was a thorough mess.

I cleaned her off somewhat, we let her into the back porch and fed her, then I took her to the brooder house for the night. No loafing under the bench in the living room, and no family and fireside that evening. Off to bed she went, unwillingly but without too much complaint. She barked once or twice, but that was all. She was tired enough to sleep, and apparently she went to sleep very soon.

That evening Barbara called Carol to ask a few questions about Penny's habits. Yes, Carol said, Penny was easily embarrassed, and when that happens she usually goes off somewhere and sulks for hours. Tender feelings, in other words. Also, that she had a sweet tooth, would eat almost anything that had sugar on or in it. And, finally, yes, they missed her, but they were glad to be rid of the responsibility of a dog that might bite other people's children. "You never know, when a dog gets that way, when it may turn on you. Or the baby, of course."

And that seemed to be that. Penny was embarrassed, you

might say, by her accident down at the cabin. She wet the floor, and she knew that was forbidden. So when she got home to the farm she took off and was gone three hours. Sulked, maybe. Or maybe she just ran the rebellion out of her, soaked it out in the mudholes and came home a tired, dirty mess.

She went to sleep, and we did too soon after. About eleven-thirty she wakened me with frantic barking, just as she had barked the night the loud-radio moron came past. I went to an open window and advised her to calm down. She did. I was so surprised, and so doubtful that it was more than a brief pause, that I lay awake almost an hour waiting for her to start up again. She never did. I finally went to sleep and slept the rest of the night.

Eight ⏤

Then began several weeks of relative quiet. Penny seemed to have got most of the contrariness, or whatever it was, out of her system. She ate like a starved child for another week or so, one day stowing away five cans of dog food before she had as much as she could hold. Her capacity was incredible. But after that spree she eased off to two cans of dog food a day, with two snacks of kibbled dry food, for another ten days. And finally she got down to normal rations, two meals a day, one a can of dog food, the other a bowlful of kibbles moistened with milk.

She went down to the lake with us one more time but was obviously so bored and unhappy there, and so nervous about that deck and the sight of the sailboat, that we tried leaving her loose at the farm. That was just what she wanted. We went down to the lake nearly every afternoon, leaving her on the front steps. When we got home, at suppertime, she was here waiting for us, as glad to see us as though we had been gone a week. Usually she went for a prowl on the mountainside after we got home. Perhaps she also went while we were away; I never found out what she did. At least, she never seemed to get into mischief or wander far. With one exception.

That exception occurred just two weeks after we brought her home to stay. We had been down at the lake that afternoon, and when we got home Penny was missing. No sound of her on the mountain. No sign of her anywhere. I wasn't worried, though I was surprised. We kept watching and listening for her. Then, about six-thirty, the phone rang. It was Carol. Penny was at her house, had been for several hours. Carol had tried several times to reach us, but there was no answer. Barbara said we would be right over.

We went, and we found Penny tied up at the garage. She was whining-happy to see us, begged to be let into the car. Carol said she just appeared out of nowhere in the middle of the afternoon. She looked out the window and saw Penny playing with the neighborhood children and couldn't believe

it. So she went out and called, Penny came to her and she
tied her up.

We brought Penny home, gave her her supper, ate ours,
and she napped in her favorite place till nine o'clock, then
went to bed quietly. We left her loose the next afternoon, as
usual, and she was lying on the front steps when we came
back from the lake.

But there were other happenings, such as the big thunderstorm. It came up a week or so later, in early afternoon. The
sky had been so ominous that we waited at home instead
of going to the lake. And a good thing we did, for it blew
madly at the lake, we were told later. Here at the farm it
was a typical explosive thunderstorm, and before it broke
both Barbara and Penny were taut and jumpy.

Barbara was apprehensive when the big, dark cloud began
to rise in the northeast. Then she saw how nervous Penny
was and she exclaimed, "You feel it too, don't you, Penny?
Well, we'll just console each other. It's good to have someone
else who knows a storm is coming."

We were all out on the front porch watching that big
cloud, black as a crow's wing. But Penny wanted in the
house. I let her in. Barbara stayed out on the porch with me
a few minutes longer, but she too was nervous, keyed up.
She asked, "Is it going to be a bad storm?" then went indoors before I could answer.

There was a low, distant rumble of thunder. The cloud
was rising swiftly. It covered almost half the sky. There was
a flicker of lightning on the horizon and, almost half a minute
later, another roll of thunder, far off. Barbara came to the
door and said, through the screen, "Penny feels it, just the

way I do." The words were hardly spoken when a flash of lightning nearby seared the sky, and less than ten seconds later a crash of thunder bounded from hill to hill and seemed to shake the very rocks.

The dark cloud was boiling now, and I looked for the green that could mean hail or the twist that could shape itself into a funnel. We seldom have hail here and tornadoes are rare, but with such a storm there are always those possibilities. I saw no green and no twist, only that big, dark cloud that was ripped repeatedly by jagged lightning, followed by thunder that jolted the house and made the windows rattle.

Barbara came out onto the porch again, watched the clouds a minute or so and said, "I wish it would rain buckets and get it over with! How much longer will it be before the thunder and lightning stop?" And again she was gone before I could even say I didn't know. But almost as though in answer to her, another blast came, lightning that blinded me and, almost immediately, a crash of thunder like a gigantic explosion just across the river. A near miss.

Then I heard the roar. It was uncanny after the silence, a silence so deep you could hear a few birds twittering out in the pasture, though there hadn't been a bird song for half an hour. The roar was like a great rush of wind. It came from up the valley and far up on the mountain. I saw the silvery curtain. It was on the mountain, and it was up the river. I could see how it covered the trees, how it moved, coming slowly, steadily down the mountain. Then I saw it coming down the river. It came down the river with a watery roar, almost the roar of a waterfall. And the river seemed to be foaming under the silvery curtain.

PENNY

Barbara was at the door, and I said, "Here it comes! We're going to get it now!" And as though I had been prophesying, another bolt of lightning ripped the sky, so close I could hear a faint sizzling noise, and almost immediately the crash of thunder jolted the whole house. Then the silvery curtain was crossing the pasture and the river was leaping and dancing and foaming. The rain struck the house as with a million hard, wet hammers, a thunder of rain, a momentary cloudburst. And one more blast of lightning and thunder, so close together they were virtually one, whose echoes were softened and dampened by the roar of the rain.

Barbara and Penny both came out onto the porch, even while the echoes of that last terrific blast were bouncing about the hills. "Whew," Barbara said. "That was a close one. But the tension is broken. Isn't it, Penny?" And Penny looked up and wagged her tail in total and relieved agreement. Maybe Penny too had a headache, as Barbara does, when those atmospheric pressures build up to a big thunderstorm.

So we three stood there, getting slightly damp, all of us, as an occasional gust blew a sheet of rain across the porch. We watched that first terrific downpour pass. The overflow of the eavestroughs stopped and there was only the surge and gurgle in the downspouts. The lightning eased away; those terrific atmospheric tensions dissipated. And the rain slackened. The rain no longer foamed but merely dimpled all over as the raindrops fell individually. The big maples no longer roared; now their leaves pattered under the individual raindrops. The spate at the roadsides relaxed into simple rivulets as the rain diminished from a flooding downpour and began to sink into the grass and the ground.

Then the sun was out again, cutting through clouds that had faded from black to pearl gray. Every tree was spotlighted, greener than it had been in days and spangled with raindrops. The rain still falling was pure, gleaming crystal against the clear blue sky in the east.

And at last the storm ended. Penny went down and rolled in the wet grass of the lawn, leaped to her feet, shook herself vigorously and turned and looked at us still on the porch. She seemed to be saying, See, I'm not afraid of water! Not as long as I can keep my feet on the good old earth.

And Barbara said to me, "She's not as much of a comfort to me as Pat was, but she's a help."

A few days later Penny showed a playful streak that she hadn't shown since the day I bought the rawhide bone and the rubber ball for her. It was an afternoon when we didn't go down to the lake, and I was doing yard chores, mowing the grass, trimming the bushes, cleaning up the litter from the thunderstorm. Penny had been watching me but without special interest. Then I found an old red rubber ball under the bridal wreath bush and I tossed it toward the porch. Penny, on the front steps, watched the ball bounce a couple of times, then came down the steps in one leap and was after it. She chased it, caught it, threw it into the air, chased it again. She turned to watch me. But I wasn't playing games. She played by herself till she worried the ball down onto the riverbank. A final toss flung it into the river, and that was the end of the ball game.

She came back across the lawn. I had taken off my work gloves and my red beaked cap when I got around into the shade of the house. She saw them, grabbed a glove and ran with it. I tried to catch her, but it was no use. She chewed the glove, made a game of the chase, and when I quit the game she dropped the glove and dashed ahead of me to grab the cap. She got it, and I knew the cap was lost. But it was no great loss, for it was old, worn and sweat-stained. I chased her a couple of times, then went back to work. She chewed and tossed and chased and chewed again for another ten minutes. The cap was reduced to a rag and I thought she had worked out her prankishness.

I came in for a cold drink, decided to quit raking, and Barbara and I went out to sit on the porch and watch evening come. Penny had hidden the cap somewhere and came and joined us. And a few minutes later the cows started for home and the milking barn. They were Albert's cows. His farm borders ours and he leased our pastures. The cows had been on the grass since the tenth of May, the day Albert insists is the time to put cows out to pasture, no matter whether the season is early or late. It's a kind of personal tradition. Those cows had been here and had gone home to be milked every day at five o'clock. After milking they would come back, to drink spring water at the old Salisbury kettle, to lie in the grass and chew their cuds, maybe to sleep. They were big black and white Holsteins, and there were fifty-odd of them.

Penny had seen those cows every day, had watched them graze, drink, lie and chew their cuds, go home to be milked, come back for the night. She hadn't so much as sniffed at them. But for some reason, that evening she took special notice of them. She watched as they started their leisurely walk down the pasture toward home. And then, before I knew what was happening, she went down off the porch the way she had gone after that old red rubber ball. Off the porch, across the lawn, around the house into the pasture, barking furiously. The cows heard her and turned to look, possibly wondering what that little bit of a dog was making so much noise about. They stood and watched as she dashed at them. The nearest one turned and trotted away. Penny was at her heels in an instant, barking and nipping. The cow broke into an awkward lope. The others hurried after her. Penny was almost hysterical. She had put the whole herd to flight.

Play is play, and maybe it started as play, though I have my doubts. But when a dog starts chasing milk cows it is not amusing. Not in dairy country. I went after Penny, across the back yard and through the gate into the pasture. I called to her, got no response. I ordered her to come back, still got no response. The cows continued to run. Penny continued to chase them. I chased Penny.

I don't know how long I chased her, more angry every minute. She didn't stop, but finally I got close enough to make a flying leap and catch her by one hind leg. Luckily, I had brought the leash. I got it on her and told her firmly that we were going home. She insisted she was going to continue chasing those big black and white cows. I was bigger than she was. We went home, Penny holding back and complaining almost every foot of the way.

I tethered her to a ring on the front porch and sat down to catch my breath. If I had half the stamina of that dog I could build an Egyptian pyramid single-handed.

"Well," Barbara said, "you two had a nice little jog, didn't you? Do that every day and—"

"And you will be a widow."

"What do we do now?"

"Lock her up for the night."

"And tomorrow?"

"I can't think that far ahead."

"Maybe she'll have forgotten all about the cows by tomorrow."

"Want to bet? When it comes to deviltry, that dog has a memory that makes an elephant look absent-minded."

As soon as I stopped puffing I took Penny to her house and locked her in, two hours early. She didn't like it. But she must have known she wasn't in high favor, because her heart really wasn't in her complaints. She yowled for twenty minutes, then shut up.

The next morning she seemed to be her usual self, greeted me happily when I let her out, ate her breakfast, went out for a little while, came back in, a model of good behavior. When I came up to my study she came along and lay here for an hour while I worked at the typewriter, then went downstairs in midmorning and went outside and lay on the front steps. The cows were in the pasture, and soon after she went outdoors they came to the watering trough to drink. I watched and saw Penny give them one uninterested look, then pay no more attention. She seemed to be thinking, *Cows? So what?* And I wondered if what happened the evening before had been just one of those things, a sudden impulse that wouldn't be repeated.

I went back to work. Nothing happened. The day passed peacefully. Late afternoon and we were on the porch again, and at five o'clock the cows began lining out for home and milking. Penny saw them, watched for a minute, got to her feet.

"Penny," I warned.

She glanced at me and turned toward the steps.

"Penny, come back here!"

I grabbed at her, but too late. She scuttled down the steps and raced across the yard toward the pasture. I picked up the leash and ran after her. The cows saw her coming and turned and loped away. Penny yelped in high triumph and took off after them. I crawled through the wire fence and followed.

It didn't take quite as long to catch her that time. The cows didn't run quite as fast. I kept hoping one of them would give Penny a kick that would send her sprawling, but it didn't happen. It might have made her all the more determined, though. I finally caught her, snapped the leash on her collar and headed for home. She didn't make half the struggle that she had the evening before. I took her home and locked her up and let her yowl. An hour later I took a can of dog food out there and gave her her supper in jail. She didn't appreciate it.

While Barbara and I ate our supper we discussed the problem.

"There must be some way," Barbara said, "to break her of chasing cows. You can break a dog of chasing cars, can't you?"

"Some dogs. Some are slow learners. They get killed."

"Penny is bright."

"Too bright for her own good."

"She should be a quick learner."

"Want to try teaching her?"

"I wouldn't know where to start."

"Well, first you learn to talk dog."

"Umm-hm. Second?"

"Get Penny to listen while you talk to her."

Barbara thought for a long moment. "Any other bright ideas?"

"Learn to talk cow."

"Yes?"

"And tell a couple of those old milkers to stop running from Penny. Tell them to kick the stuffing out of her, though I'm not sure that would do much good."

"It wouldn't. It would just make Penny mad. Now it's just a game with her, like chasing a ball. If a cow kicked her it would turn into a feud."

We let it go at that. But half an hour later Barbara called the basset owner up in Massachusetts who had given the basic advice about caring for Penny even before she came to live with us. Barbara told her about the cow problem.

"The obvious solution," Sybil said, "is to get rid of the cows."

"Yes. But what is the sensible solution. We don't even own the cows, so we can't sell them, even to please Penny."

"Well, why not put her on a leash and take her out among the cows and show her that they don't have to be chased?"

"But she doesn't chase them any other time of day. Just in the evening. She doesn't pay any attention to them in the morning. They come up here every morning and she couldn't care less."

"She sounds neurotic, to me."

"Do you know a good dog psychiatrist?"

"Look," Sybil said at last, "why don't you bring her up here to me, if she won't handle. We haven't any cows. Maybe that's the solution."

"You'd be surprised if we took you up on that."

"No, I mean it. I can find her a good home."

"We'll have to think about it." And Barbara hung up.

Nine ᥈᥈ᥩ

The next day Penny left the cows strictly alone.
We stayed at home and watched her, just to see what she
did. She was a model dog, came when called, ate her food,
didn't chase cows and went to bed without protest. The same
the next day, and the next.

Barbara said, "She's settling down, at last."

And when this exemplary behavior continued for a week

I said, "Well, life may be dull around here, but it's worth living again."

"After what we've been through with that dog," Barbara said, "I could do with weeks and weeks of this kind of dullness."

Penny was on her best behavior right through the second week, ebullient, lively, but starting no uproars. Maybe, I thought, she had finally got all that out of her system. Barbara and I both began to relax.

Looking back later, we wondered why we were surprised that it didn't last. Some dogs, like some people, simply can't abide a quiet life. Life isn't life for them unless things are happening. Maybe they have a heightened sense of drama and adventure. Maybe they actually need dragons at every turn in the road. Penny had her dragons out there in the pasture at five o'clock in the afternoon, for a few days. Then they stopped being dragons and were just plain cows. But there had to be other dragons somewhere.

It started like another normal, quiet day. Penny was her gay, happy self when I let her out of her house, frolicking and romping in the dewy grass, dashing to the back door to be let in, eating her breakfast with gusto, then going outdoors for fifteen minutes. She came back in, greeted Barbara, came up to my study with me and napped for an hour, then went down to lie on the front steps and watch the morning. All routine. Before lunch we would go for a walk, all three of us, and maybe Penny would chase a rabbit.

I was at work at my desk when a highway truck came up the road about nine-thirty. The town highway department was going to sweep our secondary blacktop road, prepare it for a coat of road oil. The highway crew is a group of men

104

we know, men who patch the chuckholes in the spring, mow
the roadsides in the summer, plow the snow in the winter.
Friends. They knew us. They knew Penny, at least by sight.

The truck came up the road, and I heard Penny bark. Then
a frenzy of barking. Then men's laughter.

I went downstairs, and there Penny was, out in the road,
disputing the way with that big red highway truck. The
driver had stopped, not wanting to run her down, and he
and the two other men with him were trying to talk her
into reason, laughing loudly all the while. Penny would back
away, they would start the truck, and she would dart in front
of it again and they would stop.

I went out, gave sharp orders, finally caught Penny by the
collar and hauled her aside so the truck could go on up the
road. I carefully explained to her that these men were
friends, that they had business on this road and that she
should shut up and lie down or she would be in trouble. She
seemed to listen. She lay down on the porch steps as though
ready to take a nap, and I went back to my typewriter.

Ten minutes later here came the sweeper, a big, unlikely
looking vehicle with revolving brushes three feet in diameter,
which sweeps the loose sand into a windrow at the edge of
the road. It came slowly up the road, grumbling and swish-
ing, and I knew there was going to be trouble even before I
heard Penny's first excited yelp. I was halfway downstairs
when she charged across the front yard and challenged that
rumbling monster. She rushed it, barking madly, threatening
to chew it into little tiny pieces.

I got out onto the porch just as the sweeper's driver
brought it to a halt in front of the house. He sat there, high
on its back, and laughed as Penny danced wildly about the

105

machine, yelping, threatening, almost hysterical. I shouted
at her, but it was no use. She couldn't hear me, even if she
had listened, above her own noise. I picked up the leash
and started across the yard, hoping to catch her before she
knew I was there. Just then the big truck came back down
the road, and for a moment Penny gave it her attention. The
sweeper's driver started up again, and she returned to that
engagement. The sweeper's driver stopped. "Go ahead!" I
shouted. "Run her down if she doesn't get out of the way!"

He shook his head and shouted back, "If she gets too
close, this thing will pick her right up, probably tear her
to pieces."

I chased her. She ran around the sweeper. I ran after her.
The truck driver stopped, and he and his helpers joined me
in the chase. We thought we had her cornered, but she
scooted between one man's legs. I followed her back toward
the house, thinking we had won, even without a capture. The
men returned to their truck. But at the porch Penny turned,
darted away from me and returned to her attack on the
sweeper.

"I'll be right back," I shouted, and came into the house,
got a length of nylon clothesline, made a loop and returned
to the road with a makeshift lasso. It was like lassoing a
snake, she was so quick and so sinuous, but I finally got the
loop on her and dragged her away. The road men shouted
their thanks and went about their business.

I brought Penny upstairs to my study and closed the door.
She whined and whimpered, threatened and entreated, for
maybe ten minutes. Then she gave up and lay down. I heard
the road truck come up the road again, and she lifted her

head, perked her ears and growled. But after that she relaxed, lay back and napped. I finished my morning's work
and took her downstairs with me. She seemed to have
quieted down completely, but I put a leash on her and
hooked it to the ring on the front porch. She lay down on the
front steps as though nothing had happened.

We had lunch, and I decided that Penny had her world
well in place again. I took off the leash, left her there on the
front porch, and within ten minutes the uproar started again.
I thought at first that the sweeper had come back, but this
time it was a horse, a horse and a big white dog. Cathy, a
teen-ager from down the road, had ridden up to discuss a
job with Barbara, and her old white collie had come with
her.

Penny had seen that horse, Cathy on him, and that old
collie at least a dozen times. Never before had she so much
as yipped at them. Now she yammered almost the way she
had at the sweeper. The horse paid little attention. Cathy
laughed and said, "Oh, Penny, what's the matter with you?
You know me." The old collie tried to ignore Penny, finally
looked down his long nose at her as though saying, What a
noisy little snippet you are. But the ruckus had to be
stopped, so I went out and collared Penny, put her on the
leash again and tethered her at the porch. Fifteen minutes
later Cathy rode back down the road and Penny didn't even
look up.

We had to go to the village to do some marketing, and I
left Penny still tethered, not wanting her to take after the
highway truck or the sweeper if they came back down the
road while we were gone. Apparently they passed before

we got home, probably without a yip out of her. She was sound asleep, the picture of innocence, when we arrived.

I let her off the leash and we came into the house. Before I had even set down the bag of groceries I heard an uproar, a typical Penny performance, out at the watering trough. Half a dozen cows were there drinking, and Penny was trying to frighten them off. It was the first time she had tried that. But the cows didn't panic. They drank their fill, then left the trough. She kept trying to put them to flight. I went out, tried to catch her, and couldn't. Since the cows weren't galloping madly away from her, I came back into the house, fed up with her antics.

I hadn't been in the house two minutes when the barking stopped. I went to the door, and there was Penny on the front porch, panting and acting innocent as a baby. I went back to the kitchen and said, "I begin to wonder just whom she is badgering, the cows or me."

"Whoever she is badgering," Barbara said, "I am getting very, very tired of it."

But there wasn't another sound out of Penny the rest of the afternoon and early evening. The cows went home undisturbed to be milked. They came back without a yelp from Penny. She ate her supper and lay on the front steps for an hour while we sat on the porch in the dusk, counting fireflies and watching the first stars appear. Then it was her bedtime.

I called her and we started to the brooder house. Just beyond the back yard, in the home pasture, were the cows, grazing as usual and moving around in the dimness of late dusk. I could make them out as dark shapes with white markings, and I could hear them grunt and wheeze and hear their hooves click as they walked. Penny and I got halfway to the brooder house, and she yelped once, charged under the fence into the pasture and was off on another of her chase-the-cows sprees.

I followed Penny and the cows clear across the pasture, back toward the road, across the pasture again, a good half mile. Then, puffing with anger as well as exertion, I paused long enough to remember the uproar at the watering trough and how Penny stopped it when I stopped chasing her.

I turned around, right there, and came back toward the house. Penny was still barking madly and the cows were running with a rumble of hoofbeats when I turned, but before I had walked a hundred yards Penny's barking began to subside. I reached the gate and came into the back yard. Penny had stopped barking, seemed to be waiting for me to catch up. Then she barked again and I heard the cows running. I came to the back door and there was another pause, another silence. Then more barking. But not frantic. Now it was almost down to the level of token barking, the kind any dog does to hear the echo. I came into the house, started to tell Barbara what had happened, and before I had finished Penny was at the front door, where she always whined when she wanted to be let in.

That time I put a leash on her and took her to the brooder house without any trouble. When I came back, Barbara said, "That settles it."

"What?"

"I've just about had it, with that dog."

"It has been quite a day, hasn't it?"

"I don't intend to live in this kind of uproar."

"It has its strenuous moments."

But she wasn't just talking. "That dog," she said, "demands excitement. She can't live more than a week or two without it. You and I can live very well with just the normal day-to-day excitement of ordinary living. Right?"

"Right. But Penny likes to be where the action is."

"Penny insists on *creating* the action. The highway truck. The sweeper. Cathy's horse. The cows at the watering trough. *And* the cows in the pasture just now. All in one day!"

"She might have spaced things out a little."

"Are you defending her?"

"Why should I defend your dog?"

"*My* dog?"

"She was a birthday present to you. She presented herself, but it was your birthday, just the same. And—"

"She is incorrigible! Worse than that car-chasing mutt down the road!"

"She feels the same way about thunderstorms—"

"Even an incorrigible child has a likable trait or two. But even with such a child, you have to do something eventually. . . . No, I've just about had it with her. Fun and games is one thing, but—" She shook her head.

"I thought she was beginning to settle down."

"I *hoped* she was, but—" And suddenly she demanded, "Why? Why does she do these things?"

"Let's wait and see what happens tomorrow."

"Want to bet?"

"No. But—she is your dog. Registered in your name."

"I should be sentimental about her?"

I didn't answer. She was being sentimental, and I knew it.

She was practically saying to Penny: *Give me back my heart. I gave it to you, but now I must have it back. Give it to me before I have to take it.*

We waited. We went to bed to sleep on the Penny problem. When I let her out the next morning she was her very best self. She romped, rolled in the damp grass, raced around me. She came to the back door and came in for her breakfast. She ate as a dog should eat. She went out and barked once or twice at the morning, wandered down the road a little way, came back and lay down on the front steps.

Midmorning and I had to do some weeding in the vegetable garden. She went to the garden with me, lay in the path and watched me work for a time. Then she grew restless, left the garden, watched the road. But no truck or sweeper was coming. She turned toward the mountain, stood there as though pondering, then took off across the pasture. I heard her up there on the mountain the better part of an hour. Then she came back, tired and wet with dew from the tall grass and underbrush.

I was still weeding. She came into the garden again and lay in the path and licked herself clean and dry. Then she went out, restless, and wandered up the road. Ten minutes and I heard her barking. Two highway trucks had gone up while she was on the mountain, and now she had found them. She yammered at them for some time. Then they came back down the road, driving slowly and carefully. Penny raced alongside, barking madly, first at one, then at the other. The driver of the lead truck slowed up beside the garden and yelled at me, with a grin, "Call off your dog. She's getting laryngitis!"

"I hope it turns to pneumonia!" I shouted back.

He grinned and drove on. The second truck followed. Penny ran alongside, barking furiously, for a couple hundred yards. Then she stopped, looked back toward the garden—and me—barked another time or two and came trotting back home. She came into the garden, lay down in the path, panting, and watched me as though expecting either praise or censure. Some reaction. I ignored her. After a few minutes she got up and left, went around the house toward the barn and the watering trough. The cows had come up the pasture while she was chasing the trucks and were at the trough, drinking.

I heard the uproar start, Penny's frantic barking. Then the sound of running cows. They came around the barn and down the pasture, fifteen or twenty of them, with Penny at their heels. The chase was on. Penny was making enough uproar for a whole pack of dogs.

I continued weeding, hoping she would stop if I didn't chase her or order her to come back. But she kept on. After a few minutes I knew it was hopeless. I quit weeding and went to the house.

Barbara met me at the door. She had heard the uproar.

"All right," I said. "You win the bet. How much was it?"

"A million dollars. . . . Shall I call Sybil?"

"Not until Penny tires of this nonsense for five minutes and I can get a leash on her."

"I think she is stopping now."

I listened. All was quiet in the home pasture. I got the leash, went to the front door and waited, perhaps another five minutes. Then here she came, panting, looking almost smug and triumphant. She came up the steps, saw me in the

112

doorway, hesitated, then flopped down on the porch and looked up at me with what seemed an almost malicious, defiant grimace. I went out and snapped the leash on her collar, fastened the other end to the ring on the porch post.

I came back in and said, "First I want to call Tom or Carol."

Carol answered. Tom was at work. I asked her if Pokey-Penny ever chased cars while they had her. Carol hesitated. "Well," she finally said, "yes. Toward the end she began to chase cars and trucks. I thought she did it just to plague me, but Tom said she would get over it. He scolded her, but it didn't do much good. That's the main reason we tied her up. And then she began snapping at the kids."

"Did she chase cows?"

"I don't think she ever saw a cow till she went over to your place."

"Would you take her back?"

"No. Tom told you that."

"I thought you might have changed your minds."

"No."

"We may have to give her away."

"That's all right. I don't want her back, ever."

"Thanks. Tell Tom what I said, will you?"

"I'll tell him."

I hung up and told Barbara to call Sybil whenever she wanted to. She said, "Why wait?" and put in the call, got Sybil at once. Yes, Sybil said, her offer was still good. Bring Penny up and she would find a good home for her, where there weren't any cows or highway trucks. She gave directions for reaching her place.

It was almost lunchtime. Barbara started putting things

on the table. I opened a can of dog food, put the contents in Penny's dish.

"She had her morning meal," Barbara said.

"The condemned prisoner always gets a last meal."

"This isn't an execution, for goodness sake!"

"Just banishment. But she gets that last meal, just the same."

"Now who's being sentimental?"

We ate, and Penny ate. I got out the car. Penny loved to ride in the car. She was eager to get in, but I kept her on the leash, tethered. I didn't want her kiting off and making me chase her for half an hour.

"All set," I called from the front door.

"I'll be another ten minutes."

"Why?"

"I'm getting the dog food together. We're going to take it along, every bit of it, and give it to Sybil."

So I waited, and I took the carton of canned and kibbled dog food out and stowed it in the car trunk. Then I put Penny in the car. Barbara was ready. We headed up the road.

Penny was as excited as a child going to the circus. She watched the roadside, sniffed at the dogs we passed, perked her ears and wrinkled her nose at the cats.

"I feel," Barbara said, "like a—a scapegoat. Or whatever it is that leads the sheep to slaughter."

"The Judas goat. But I believe you reminded me just a little while ago that Penny isn't going to be slaughtered. She is going to a brand new home where she can show off and get everybody's attention. For a while, at least."

After a moment Barbara said, "She *is* a lovable dog."

114

Penny sat there on the back seat, long ears pendulous, eyes innocent, sturdy legs braced, and seemed to be listening to every word. Barbara turned and put out a hand to pat her head, and Penny licked it with a slobbery tongue. Whatever lay ahead, she obviously had no qualms.

Ten ↝

Sybil's place was a gray farmhouse set well back from the road. There was a modest sign, "Antiques," at the foot of the driveway. The farm had about two hundred acres of meadow and woodland, which was managed but not farmed, and Sybil dealt in antiques more as a hobby than a business.

We drove in and parked, and I went to the side door,

rang. After a moment a dark-haired, youngish middle-aged woman came to answer. She wore dark horn-rim glasses, a pink pullover sweater, dark slacks. She invited us in, said yes, she was Sybil.

Barbara came, and I got Penny, still on the leash. At the door Sybil said, "Let her off the leash. Let her go where she wants to. She'll smell my dogs."

The entry room was a display room with low tables loaded with antique dishes and glassware. A fine place, I thought, for an exuberant dog to romp! Sybil held the door open and Penny went in, looked around, moved carefully, didn't touch a table or disturb anything. She crossed the room ahead of us to the far door. There Sybil led the way along a short hall to the living room. Dogs elsewhere in the house sensed a stranger and began to bark. Penny perked her ears, paused to look and listen, but didn't answer. But she was so excited that she spilled in the hallway. Sybil said, "It happens with any dog. Nervous, excited, in a strange place." She brought a couple of paper towels, wiped up.

Her dogs, she said, were safely in the other part of the house. Four dogs. An old female basset, a very old cocker, an old dachshund, and a young Cairn. "We'll let Abby, my basset, in pretty soon. But first we'll let Penny look around, find out where she is. After all, this is a totally strange place to her."

Barbara and I sat on the sofa, Sybil sat in a chair, and Penny looked inquiringly at an empty upholstered chair, remembered her manners and came and lay down on the rug in front of us.

"You can get in the chair, Penny," Sybil said. Then, to us, "In this house dogs can do whatever they want to. Get into any chair, go into any room, eat when they are hungry. Yes, I know it's against the rules, but that's the way we live around here. Mine aren't show dogs. They live with us, not out in kennels. We do have a big run, on the far side of the house, and it's well fenced. That's where I'll put Penny for a few days, till she gets used to the place."

"You'll find a home for her?" Barbara asked.

"Well, yes." Sybil looked at Penny, who looked back with her most appealing air. "Four dogs is plenty, even for us! My husband said just the other day that when one of the old dogs dies we won't replace it. He's away for the day. He'll be home tonight. I think I'd better put Penny out in the run before he gets home. He's a sucker for bassets." She laughed.

I gave her the papers Tom had given me. She glanced through them, nodded. "Just as I thought, there's a gap. Great-grandma must have had an affair with some wandering Lothario. A beagle, I'll bet. Penny's eyes are not quite bagged enough and her ears are just a trace too short for the perfect basset. But that's all right, Penny. We love you just the same."

We talked dogs in general while Penny relaxed. Finally Sybil said, "Well, Penny, how would you like to meet Abby? I think it's time you did. You two will have to get along somehow." She turned to us. "Abby is a dowager, and she thinks she rules the roost around here. I guess she does, at that. The other dogs let her have her way. I'll go and get her."

She went to another room and came back with Abby, a grizzled white and tan basset. She was fat, barrel-shaped. Her eyes were deeply pouched and red-rimmed. Her ears

118

almost touched the floor. She came into the room, saw Penny, stopped, looked down her nose, obviously annoyed. Young Penny got to her feet, stood in front of us, her tail slowly wagging. Then the tail stopped. Some signal passed between them. Abby took a couple of steps toward her and Penny backed away, stood at Barbara's knee. Penny growled a warning. Abby barked, a sharp, hoarse bark.

"Abby," Sybil said firmly, "now stop that. Behave yourself."

Abby paid no attention. She barked again, definitely a challenge.

I reached for Penny's collar. "No!" Sybil said. "Let her go. They have to get this over with."

Penny barked, a different bark than I had ever heard, a defiant bark. Abby snarled, chomped her jaws, barked again.

Penny moved toward the center of the room, barking steadily now, accepting the challenge. Abby took a couple of steps toward Penny, also barking. The uproar was deafening. The other dogs, behind closed doors at the far side of the house, began to bark. They knew what was happening, sensed it or perhaps knew what Abby was saying. And of course they heard Penny's voice, the voice of a stranger.

The two bassets, old dowager and young intruder, were in the center of the room, still two feet apart, Abby challenging, Penny defiant. I was on the edge of my chair, ready to leap in with that chain leash when they began to fight. Sybil sat there as taut and as ready as I was. Barbara shrank back on the couch, fascinated but dreading the clash that seemed inevitable.

Sybil was talking to them. "Abby, Abby, ease it up now,

Abby. Penny! Take it easy, Penny. Easy, easy. Now, Abby. Now, Penny." Her voice almost droned at them, soothing. But neither dog seemed to be listening.

Abby made a rush, pushed Penny with her shoulder. But she didn't nip. Teeth bared, eyes blazing, she nudged Penny again, then retreated. Penny didn't slash back, as I had thought she would. But she didn't retreat. She took the pushing, and she edged forward as Abby retreated. They were almost nose to nose. Abby retreated another step. Penny followed her, so angry now that there were flecks of white foam on her lips.

At that point Sybil stood up, said sharply, "That's enough! Shut up, both of you! Abby, be quiet! Penny, stop it! Stop it, I say!" And she stepped between them. Abby backed away, and Penny backed away. I let out a long-held breath. Sybil shooed Abby toward the door, opened it, crowded her into the other room, closed the door. She came back and sat down with a let-out breath that whistled. "Well," she said, "that's over."

Penny had come back and stood beside my knee. Her lips were still flecked with foam. She was quivering and her heart was racing; I could see the throb against her ribs. I was so proud of her I could almost have changed my mind, brought her back home. Almost.

Sybil was saying, "I guess Penny can stay. She can take care of herself."

"You're not afraid they will fight?" Barbara asked.

"I don't think they will now. They've had it out. Abby knows Penny won't be bluffed. And I think Penny knows where Abby stands around here. They'll make their peace, somehow. They may get noisy about it a few times, but I doubt that they will fight."

"I thought they'd tear each other to pieces," Barbara said. "I could see blood all over the place!"

"To tell the truth," Sybil said, "I wasn't sure myself, for a time. If Penny had snapped at her when Abby rushed her— But she didn't. Penny, you are a good dog, a very good dog. You've got the courage of a blue-ribbon basset, whether Great-grandma was indiscreet or not. In fact, I think you are quite a dog, Penny."

There wasn't much to say after that, or much reason to stay. I went out to the car and got the carton of dog food, brought it in and left it in the hallway. We talked another ten minutes and said we'd go along. I gave Sybil the leash and she put it on Penny, who seemed to have the idea that she was going with us.

As we went down the hallway, there was Abby at the box of dog food, taking a milk bone from the open box.

"Find something you like, Abby?" Sybil asked.

Abby turned and went into the other room, the milk bone in her mouth.

"One thing about Penny," Barbara said, "she doesn't snitch food. You won't have any trouble with her that way."

Sybil smiled. "As I said, the dogs around here eat whenever they think they are hungry. There's always something around for them to eat."

We went back through the display room and out to the car. Sybil came with us, and Penny, on the leash. Penny expected to get into the car, but Sybil said, "No, Penny. You are staying here. Right here, with us." We got in and closed

121

the doors, and Penny, for the first time I ever saw it, looked disappointed.

They were still standing there, Penny watching, still looking disappointed, when we looked back from the foot of the driveway. Then we were on the highway and heading home.

We drove a couple of miles before Barbara said, "Penny is going to have a lot of new experiences. She won't be bored, for a little while at least."

"Penny," I said, "is going to be a busy dog. She has to make a place for herself in a household that already has four dogs. Every one of those four is a rival."

"Do you think Sybil will find a home for her?"

"Who knows?"

"I don't think so. I'll bet Penny stays right there. She said her husband likes bassets."

"Maybe he only likes fat old bassets. Didn't Penny look young and slim beside Abby?"

"Like a puppy. Like a teen-ager!"

"And didn't she stand up to Abby's noise and bluster?"

"I thought they were going to tear each other limb from limb. I thought they were going to wreck the place."

"If Penny had snapped at Abby just once, they would really have gone at it. And I don't think Penny would have got the worst of it, either. You know, when she stood up to Abby that way I was almost sorry we were giving her away."

"Now I suppose you are going to get sentimental about her. You, the tough guy, who could take a dog or leave it go!"

"I'm not at all sentimental about her. I just admired her courage. She's gone; good riddance. She's a whimsical bitch who won't stay home, doesn't know the meaning of the word. I'm glad we took her in, and I'm glad we got rid of her."

"Well, I think I am too. I don't know. I kind of wish she would be waiting for us there on the front steps." She paused. "The way she was at first, I mean. Not the way she is now, chasing cows and trucks and raising cain just for the uproar!" Another pause. "But Penny was a darling when she was good."

"And a hellion when she was bad."

"I loved her."

I refused to commit myself. Not aloud, at least. I was the tough guy. I could take her or leave her. We had just left her. Good riddance! But she was a lot of dog, had a lot of guts.

We stopped in Barrington to buy a few groceries. But mostly to go into a store and not buy any dog food. I knew it. Barbara knew it. But neither of us said it. We walked right past the dog food shelves and didn't say a word.

We came on home, and as we came down the back road I thought: She won't be on the front steps, waiting. She won't bark the greeting bark and come down to the car, wagging from nose to tail tip, glad to see us. Then I thought: And she won't wait till we get indoors, then go out to the watering trough and chase the cows, just to create an uproar.

We pulled up in front of the garage. It was not quite four o'clock. "Let's go on down to the lake," Barbara said.

"All right, let's."

"In a few minutes. A couple of things I want to do first."

We went in the house and Barbara went to the living room, picked up the throw rug under the bench where Penny chose to lie and nap. She handed it to me. "Take it down and put it in the washer, with half a cup of detergent."

I took it down to the basement, started the washer, put

the detergent in, and the throw rug, left it to go through the full cycle. Upstairs again, I found Barbara on the back porch. "Take the blanket outdoors," she said. "Throw it over the line, let it air. We'll take it to the cleaner's tomorrow."

I took the old Navy blanket outdoors. When I came in again she had mopped the floor where Penny's food dish stood. She moved the trash basket, put it where the dish had been, handed me a big paper bag. "The dish," she said. "Put it out with the trash in the garage."

She washed her hands. "All right, let's go. Now we can come home to *our* house. After we watch the sun go down at the lake."

We drove down to the lake, to the camp. She changed to her bathing suit. I put on my trunks. We went down to the dock and sat there dangling our feet in the cool water.

"It's just about time for the cows to go home to be milked," she said.

I nodded.

"How about going for a swim with me? Feel big and strong today?"

I shivered but said yes. She let herself down into the water, pushed off from the dock. "Come on, sissy!"

I waited till she was safely away from the dock, then I dived in, the only sensible way to get into the water. Get wet all over in one big splash. I went in like a dog diving, not a porpoise, and I came up blowing and snorting. But I swam after her. I couldn't catch her, otter that she is, but I followed. Out maybe a hundred yards. Then she waited for me and we rolled over and floated. She said, after a few minutes, "She will be top dog there within a week."

"She is right now."

"And he won't let Sybil give her away."

"She'll miss the cows."

After a moment she said, "You will miss her, won't you?"

I tried to make an emphatic answer, got a mouthful of water and sputtered like a sick geyser.

"I will," she said. "You all right? Let's go back and sit in the sun. Just sit and be Indians."

I got my breath. "Indians *eat* dogs."

"We'll eat hot dogs."

We swam back to the dock and lay in the sun and dried off. And went up and lay on the chaises on the deck and didn't even want to bother to go for a sail. It was wonderful, just lying there in the late afternoon sun. After a while she went to the little kitchen and put water on to heat. When it boiled she took frankfurters from the refrigerator and put them in the pot and set it aside. I sliced and buttered buns and opened the relish. We mixed drinks and carried trays out onto the deck, where we ate and watched the sun go down, and stayed there till the first stars came out.

Then it was nine o'clock, and we got in the car and came home to the farm. Just to be coming home. And not have to chase a dog that was chasing cows. Not have to put a leash on a dog to take her out to the little brooder house for the night. Not have to get up at midnight and try to quiet her down after some idiot drove past with his radio blatting.

We came home and put the car away, and as we were walking across the lawn toward the front steps Barbara caught my hand and gripped it very hard. She didn't say a word. We stopped at the foot of the steps, and still she didn't say anything. Then she let go of my hand and reached into her pocket for a face tissue.

We went up onto the porch and I held the screen door for her. But she didn't go in. She turned and looked at the starlight in the sky to the east, and at the river beyond the road, and at the winking starlight in the river. She reached for my hand again and said, "She did come for my birthday. The day before my birthday."

"Six months ago tomorrow."

We came into the house, into the living room. I flicked on the lights and she looked at the bench against the wall. "Oh, the rug! Would you put it in the dryer? It'll be dry by morning."

When I came back we went upstairs and to bed. Lights out, I said, "You miss her, don't you?"

"Umm, yes. Don't you?"

"Nuts to Penny."

She laughed.

"What's funny?"

"You."

She was silent several minutes, then asked, "You don't suppose she can find her way back, do you?"

"Back here?"

"Yes."

"Of course she can, if she wants to. Penny can go anywhere she wants to, blindfolded. She has a built-in radar, or something."

"There are ways to jam radar, aren't there?"

"Not the kind she has. Hers is more like ESP."

"All women," she said, "have that, to some degree."

And we let it go at that.

Eleven ⁓

Penny didn't come back here the next day, or the next week. We began to relax. But I still found myself listening for her out at the watering trough or in the pasture every afternoon, and in the morning I had to check myself from going out to open the brooder house while the coffee was perking. I noticed, too, that Barbara went to the front door from time to time, glanced out at the porch, then turned away almost guiltily. And when she crossed the living room she stayed far enough away from the bench against the wall so she wouldn't step on the foot or tail that wasn't there. Down at the lake we would sit on the deck and she would stare off into space, then turn to me with a quick smile and ask, "Don't you want to go for a sail?" Then catch herself and laugh. "You *have* been out, haven't you? I must have been daydreaming."

Toward the end of the second week, when we came home from the lake she stood in the dooryard and turned and looked across the road at the river. "Isn't it peaceful? I'd almost forgotten how peaceful it really is here."

We came up onto the porch. "Some people," she said, "can't stand the quiet, I guess. They have to shout and create an uproar."

"People?"

"Well, people too." Then she asked, "Why couldn't she have settled down and enjoyed it here? Was she bored, or what?"

I hadn't any answer, but after a moment's silence I said, "Why don't you call Sybil?"

"I don't want to be a softie, but—"

"I'd like to know, too. Go ahead and call her."

She made the call while I went out to the garden and picked ripe tomatoes and late lettuce for a salad supper. She had just hung up when I came back in.

"Penny's all right," she announced. "She hasn't run away once. They still haven't found a home for her, but I'm not at all sure they really tried. Sybil kept saying what a good dog she is and how much her husband likes her. Sybil said she admires Penny. Maybe you can admire a show dog, but does anyone admire a house dog? Well, anyway, she is eating well and gets along with the other dogs. She and Abby haven't chewed each other up, at least. Sybil says Penny is very much the individual and doesn't *need* the other dogs."

"But she's still there," I said. "And Sybil didn't ask us to come take her back?"

"No. But there's something about it that I don't understand. I can't put my finger on it and I don't think Sybil can. Penny doesn't fit into the pattern up there, either, and I think Sybil is just as baffled as we were."

"Penny," I said, reaching for something I didn't really understand either, "is one of those dogs who are very amusing in retrospect, but hell on wheels while it is happening, if you know what I mean. Take the time she chased the ball in the living room. It seems very funny now."

"Not to me."

"I agree it wasn't funny at the time, though any young dog probably would have done the same thing. But I can laugh at it now. I wonder if some of the other impossible things she did won't seem funny in time."

"Chasing the cows?"

"Well, no. But it was funny when she attacked the road sweeper. I can laugh at that now."

Barbara shook her head. "It's something that goes deeper than mere clowning. Or even such an absurd stunt as attacking the sweeper. There's something almost paranoid about that. . . . Anyway, it will be very interesting to hear what happens. Something will happen, you can be sure of that."

Two more weeks, and then one evening Sybil called us.

I took the call. She didn't even mention Penny at first. She asked how we were, she discussed the weather. Finally I asked, "How is Penny?"

"Oh," she said, with a transparent air of surprise that I even mentioned the subject, "she's fine. Just fine. We got her a license. Yes, Bob fell for her, just as I thought he might. So we decided to keep her. What's one more dog, with the pack we have around here?" She laughed, a rather forced laugh. "But she has been a little restless. Last week she kited off and was gone all day. As a matter of fact, she's been gone all day today. You haven't seen anything of her, have you?"

"Not a sign."

"I didn't think so. This is home to her now. She has just gone to see one of her friends down the road, probably, and forgot to come home. She'll be back by morning. But if she should happen to—"

"We'll call you if she shows up here."

"Thanks."

We hung up, and I went to the front door to look out on the porch. Then, to make sure, I went outdoors and looked, walked around the house. When I came in I began to laugh.

"What," Barbara asked, "is so funny?" She had been upstairs while I took the call.

"Penny," I said. "And Sybil." And I told her about the call.

"Why were you laughing at Sybil just now?"

"Just on general principles. She's talking just the way we were talking six weeks ago."

We were alert all evening for that unmistakable sound on the front porch. When we went to bed I expected to be wakened at 2:00 A.M. by barking and scratching at the front door. I wasn't. I slept till 5:30, as usual, then came down-stairs in robe and slippers and looked out on the front porch before I made the coffee. No dog. I drank my coffee with a mixture of disappointment and relief. It did hurt, just a little, to think that Penny could forget us so completely. But I said nothing like that aloud, or even above the slightest whisper to myself.

There was no sign of Penny all day. But just as we were eating supper that evening the phone rang. Barbara took the call, was gone five minutes and came back to the table with the word, "Relax. She's home, at Sybil's." She sat down and told me what Sybil had said while she finished her supper.

People six miles away phoned that afternoon and said Penny was at their house. They had traced her by her license tag. She was such a sweet dog, so well-mannered and affectionate, they almost wished she was theirs. Sybil asked if they wanted her for keeps, but they said they really couldn't because they went south in the winter and couldn't take her. But she was welcome to visit them any time. So Sybil went and got her. "And," Sybil said, "this I must tell you. Penny and Abby haven't had any fights, but they have barely tolerated each other. But this afternoon when we brought her home, Abby went over to Penny and kissed her, nuzzled her with a real dog kiss. So she's one of the gang now, and I think she will stay at home."

"Sybil said that?" I asked.

"Word for word."

We looked at each other and began to laugh. Finally I asked, "What are you laughing at?"

"Sybil. I think. What are you laughing at?"

"You."

131

"All right, the things Penny does can be funny, in retrospect. Or when she pulls one on someone else. Remember the day they called us from the lime plant?"

"We went and got her, and she was absolutely white with lime dust. Looked like she had fallen into a barrel of flour."

"And she wasn't even living here. She'd gone back home."

"But still had our license tag. That's how they traced her."

We laughed again.

"Good old Penny."

"She's not old."

"Old enough to know what she's doing. Remember how she would sit on the porch or just stand in the yard, and look. Not at something, the way a normal dog does, at a leaf or a bird or a car, but just staring into space. You could almost see those little wheels going round in her head, thinking up some new deviltry. Maybe just a romp up the mountain, but even that meant a chance to wallow in every seep spring up there."

"Well, at least she went back to Sybil's."

"They went and got her."

"She stayed up in that area."

"She didn't *want* to come back down here."

"I suppose your feelings are hurt."

"I'm wounded to the quick. Let's celebrate."

Mid-October came and the leaves reached the peak of their color here in the hills. The autumn wanderlust, restless counterpart of spring fever, made it hard to stay indoors or even at home. If I were a dog with an itchy foot, October is the time when I certainly would light out.

I watched the front porch every morning, as soon as I got

up. But she didn't come. The air was balmy by day, frosty
by night. There was brilliance in the trees, crispness underfoot. The air smelled of ripeness, of butternut hulls, of purple
grapes that the possums fed on every night, of fermenting
windfall apples, of minty bee balm at the roadside. Asters
and bouncing Bet whitened the roadsides, and lavendered
and purpled them, and in hidden, unexpected places the
gentians spread their incredible blueness and faded. Flickers
gathered in restless flocks. Milkweed floss spilled from the
pods, thistledown was dragged from the heads by the gold-
finches, and silvered the breeze and went shimmering off
toward the horizon. Bittersweet berries split their tan husks
and shone in their orange brightness. 'Coons were busy in
the cornfields every night, cottontails were all over the place,
woodchucks were waddly with fat stored for their long
winter sleep. Ruffed grouse, which we simply call "birds,"
feasted in the wild barberry tangles, and when you walked
in the woods they flew from underfoot with a roar that
startled you half out of your wits. Foxes were abroad every
night and occasionally in the autumn-misted dawn.

As I said, if I were a dog I would have to get out and
go when the year reaches that point. As a man, I had to go
and look at the far side of a few hills. So we went, driving
the back roads and the country lanes whenever we could.
But we kept well away from Sybil's area. If Penny was out
autumn-wanderlusting, we didn't want to cross her path. So
we went on one-day trips all through the superb days of
Indian summer. Then it turned dour and wet. The rain
brought down most of the leaves. We stayed at home till
the sky cleared, then made one more excursion to see the far
horizon, which is so much wider after the leaves have fallen.

133

Then we went over to the lake and closed things up for the winter, and here at the farm we did all the autumn chores and, in a sense, began to snug in for the winter. We had firelight evenings, the time when country folk are glad they have four walls, a pantry, a root cellar and a woodpile. We began to settle into the annual status of indoor people, though we probably wouldn't have more than a light snow until after Thanksgiving, with luck not till after Christmas.

The week of Thanksgiving a letter came from Sybil.

"Just a report," she wrote. "I thought you might like to know how Penny is doing. Well, she is doing pretty much as she pleases. But we get along. I guess I didn't tell you, but she had an encounter with a porcupine. She found one back in our woods and, being Penny, had to try to scare it off. You know porkies. Penny got a whole mouthful of quills. We had to take her to the vet and he knocked her out to get all the quills, and kept her overnight. She came home cocky as ever, but she did have a sore mouth for a few days and was picky about her eating. But she learned a lesson. She's smart. She hasn't got into a porcupine since, though she has been out in the woods several nights. That's the way she is. She decides she isn't going to stay here, so she goes somewhere. She comes home when she feels like it. Or we go and get her. By now, folks know her for ten or twelve miles around. She goes and visits them, and when they get tired of her they call us. And I'll have you know that now she has a pass on the school bus. If she's out somewhere and wants to come home, she waits at a school bus stop and gets on when the bus comes along. The driver knows her, and so do the kids. They bring her right to our driveway.

"I could go on and on about her. There's only one black

mark against her. She doesn't like my cat. They don't actually fight, but Penny doesn't like cats and that's that. On the
other hand, she does like our big white rabbit. You know
how she chases cottontails. Well, the other day, when Penny
was home, she was asleep on her blanket in the kitchen, and
the white rabbit was let loose in there. It's the rabbit's
kitchen too, of course. Well, Penny sensed it, I guess, because she opened one eye and saw this big white creature,
and looked again, practically bug-eyed. She sat up, and
then she went over to the rabbit, and the rabbit just twitched
its nose and stared back. And Penny practically said, Hello,
I'm glad to know you. The rabbit waggled its ears and Penny
almost smiled. Then she went back and lay down and went
to sleep. So maybe it evens out, cat and rabbit.

"I could go on and on, but I won't. I admire Penny. She's
a free soul. She's going to live life the way she wants it, and
that's that. Right now she's gone for the day, but she'll be
back. Tonight or tomorrow. Probably tonight she'll come
and bark under my window, and I'll get up and let her in.
Come up and see us. Let me know ahead of time and I'll
make sure she's here. . . . Sybil."

We read the letter through and Barbara said, "It's fascinating for what she doesn't say."

"I wish Penny would write and tell us her side of the
story."

"I know what Penny would say."

"What?"

"She would say, 'Life is really good. I've found someone
who lets me do exactly as I please. I would anyway,' she
would say, 'but it's nicer when people don't make a fuss and
try to force me to live by rules.'"

135

"Penny wants to make the rules."

"If there have to be rules, yes. . . . I think I understand what Sybil means when she says she admires Penny. Deep down, most of us would like to make the rules. Or ignore them. Some of the time at least."

"Who makes these rules?"

"Society. Civilization, I suppose. Society demands that you follow patterns. Otherwise there would be chaos, anarchy."

I agreed. There are times when most of us feel like rebelling, especially when we are young. Before we have settled, or been forced, into the mold of conformity. The ideal, of course, would be a world where no rules are needed, and that is the Utopian dream, basically. The trouble, of course, is that before long a new set of rules emerges, based on the tenet: Thou shalt not obey the old rules. And there goes Utopia, in another code of "Thou shalt's."

"That's a fine theory," I said, "the make-your-own-rules idea. But it doesn't make the rule-maker easy to live with."

"That," Barbara said, "is one of the rules that have to be broken right at the start—'Thou shalt be easy to live with.' Break that one, and go on from there with an easy conscience. Penny obviously does."

"And comes out where?"

"A free soul, as Sybil says. Sybil doesn't know what to do about that either. We tried, and we couldn't find the answer. Sybil admires her and lets her go her own way. Maybe that's the answer."

December passed with just enough snow to cover the ground. After Christmas, January brought a storm that left two-foot drifts and subzero temperatures. Not the kind of weather that invites even restless dogs to go wandering. We wondered if Penny had settled in and become a tractable house dog, but we had no word from Sybil and we didn't call to ask. As the weeks passed, our concern for Penny lost its intensity. She had a home where she was cosied and cared for, and she had people who admired, and tolerated, her independence. She evidently had friends all over that area who welcomed her whenever she went visiting. She was a privileged individual. We were only a couple of people she had known in passing, you might say: acquaintances, good to know. So the ties of affection were loosened in us and began to fall away.

February was blustery, as usual, and March came in like the proverbial lion. But soon after the vernal equinox it quieted down to the lamblike temper that can make an occasional New England spring a delightful surprise. Usually we have little or no spring; we go from late winter right into summer, with maybe a couple of mild days between. But this year the tree frogs were yelping by the last week in March, the pussy willows were fat and furry, and the migrant robins were back in our pastures, great flocks of them, and the redwing blackbirds *ka-reed* from the trees along the river. Spring's outriders arrived and we welcomed them with open arms. A benevolent April is an event here. We don't so much expect April showers to bring May flowers; we only hope April showers won't turn into sleet storms or snow, and we expect the May flowers to take care of themselves. They always do, even though we nearly always have hard frost right up till the end of the month. We have had snow in May, and we have had killing frost the first week in June.

But that year April was gentle and May was balmy. We

got the vegetable garden planted. We opened the place at the lake and we watched the water temperature there. This looked like an early swimming year. We had worked all winter, finished one book, got a start on another. We could take time off that summer. We came up to Memorial Day with things well in hand. Then Barbara said, "I wonder when Penny is going to arrive."

"What?"

"Don't tell me you have forgotten already."

"I had pretty well put her out of my mind, yes. Till you brought the matter up."

"This is fine traveling weather. Just about a year ago now she was coming and going from here."

"I would just as soon let sleeping dogs lie."

So we went to the lake and she had her first swim. I put the sailboat in the water. When we got home that evening she said, "I'm going to call Sybil."

They talked almost twenty minutes. When she had hung up, Barbara said, "I think we are safe. But apparently it was quite a winter, up there."

Penny, it seems, discovered a ski slope a few miles down the road. She found that many youngsters were there on weekends, subteen-agers who came by bus Friday evening and were on the slopes all day Saturday. Most of them were novices learning to ski. Penny took to going down there Friday afternoons, meeting the bus, spending the night at the ski lodge, then having an all-day romp Saturday. The youngsters rode the ski tow and Penny ran up the slope after them. When they skied down she dashed right along, often underfoot. She accounted for dozens of spills but, miraculously, for no broken bones. The children loved her. The cook at the lodge fed her salami sandwiches. Evenings she stretched out in front of the big fireplace and napped. When the youngsters went to bed she went along and crawled in with one little girl or another.

Sybil went down there after her one Saturday and said, "There she was, walking around the ski lodge as though she owned the place. With that princess air. She wouldn't even look at me. I had to put a leash on her to get her out of there, and if I hadn't locked the door when I got her home she'd have gone right back."

Some weekends, of course, she passed up the ski lodge. She needed variety. There were five or six houses that she visited more or less regularly for a meal and a bed, and if the accommodations were particularly good she often stayed several nights. And once she went out into the woods and spent two nights, bitter nights, well below zero. Sybil and Bob heard her baying, but when they went to look for her she kept quiet and they never found her. After the second night she came home, limping, with one forepaw frostbitten. It healed all right, but it was sore for a couple of weeks and she didn't travel.

She made friends with the rural mail carrier. It was while she was lame. She went out to the main road, probably hoping someone would give her a ride. The mailman came along, stopped at a box, and there was Penny, practically begging, looking downright pathetic. He let her in his car and she rode the rest of his route and went back to the post office with him. There the postmaster checked her license and phoned Sybil, told her he had a special delivery package she'd better come and get. Sybil asked why, and he said there was postage due. "Postage due!" she exclaimed. "Send it back!" "It's just one penny," he said, laughing. And Sybil went and got her.

"Penny," Sybil summed up to Barbara, "is completely blithe. She's going to have to pay the price, some day, I suppose. But meanwhile she's going to live the way she wants to. This morning she wanted out, and she just sat there on the lawn and looked, this way and that, and you could almost hear her saying to herself, Well, this is a warm, inviting day. Something exciting will turn up, if I just go somewhere. And pretty soon she took off. I don't know where she went, and she's still gone. But I've stopped worrying about her. She'll come back when she gets good and ready."

Twelve ~

It was a quiet summer. The memory of Penny didn't vanish like morning mist, but we did stop looking out the front door to see if she was on the front porch and we no longer walked wide of the bench in the living room. Sybil hadn't phoned or written and Barbara hadn't called Sybil since the first week in May.

Labor Day passed, and there we were in September, practically in autumn. Barbara said, "It's been a year now. A little over a year."

"What's been a year?"

"Since Penny left."

"Oh. You mean since Penny was given her walking papers, as my grandmother used to say."

"What does that mean?"

"It means scram, scat, go on away, get lost."

"Still mad at Penny, aren't you?"

"No. How can anybody be mad at a free soul? At freedom?"

"I'd like to call Sybil."

"Go ahead. But for heaven's sake, don't wish Penny any happy returns."

I went out and sat on the front steps while she made the call, listening to the whippoorwills on the mountainside, watching the slow current of the river. When she had finished, she came out and sat down beside me.

"Situation pretty much unchanged," she reported. "Penny goes and comes pretty much as she pleases. A little while back she spent a week with folks five or six miles away, and they said they would like to keep her. Sybil agreed, but just a few days later she was back at Sybil's. The minute those folks treated her as though she was theirs, instead of an honored guest, she walked out."

"Princess Penny."

"Sybil says folks call her Agent Seventy-seven. That's her tag number, and apparently it's known all over the area. In July she vanished for almost a week, and then Sybil had a call from a horse farm twenty-odd miles away. Penny was there, hobnobbing with the horses. Loved horses, the man said. Sybil went down and got her and she's stayed close to home since."

"Meaning that she's there from time to time?"

"I suppose so. Sybil asked us up."

"When?"

"Any time."

"Why? Anything special?"

"To see Penny. To see if she still knows us. Sybil says she has changed, grown up."

"To see if we won't take her back."

"Oh, for goodness sake! Sybil's not trying to get rid of Penny."

"Of course not. Sybil admires Penny. . . . When do you want to go?"

"Not this week. Maybe next. I told her we'd phone a day ahead, so she could make sure Penny is there."

Ten days later Barbara phoned Sybil, said we planned to go up there the next day. "That'll be just fine," Sybil said. "I'll be here, and Penny's here. I'll keep her in. Lucky you didn't call earlier. She's been gone two days and didn't get home till about an hour ago. . . . We'll see you tomorrow."

It was a bright, sunny, late-September day. The color had begun to come in the trees, the swamp maples fiery red in places, the sumac marching along the back roads like Indians in scarlet feather headdresses. The aspens and the gray birches were greenish gold, making the hillsides shimmer. And the asters were everywhere, whitening the roadsides and frosting the old meadows, with here and there a brilliant patch of the big purple New England asters with their rich yellow centers, the royalty of the whole aster family. The blue jays looked twice as blue as they had all summer, somehow reflecting the blue of the autumn sky, and the crows were black as sin.

"What a beautiful day!" Barbara exclaimed. "And Penny is being kept in. I'll bet she's fit to be tied."

"If Sybil is at all bright, Penny *is* tied. . . . Think she will know you?"

"Of course she will."

We passed Barrington and headed northeast on the winding, hill-country road. Finally we climbed to a plateau and the road leveled out somewhat, with reclaimed farmhouses here and there, most of them closed for the winter. Next April they would begin to come to life again, and after a month or two of weekending they would come to life with summer animation, with women and children and dogs, and with men on weekends. Several of them, nicely restored old country houses, had swimming pools in their side yards, strange substitutes for the woodsheds and privies that had been there originally. Only a few of the houses, occupied by year-rounders, showed signs of life, smoke from a chimney, a car parked in the driveway, open garage doors. None of those occupied houses seemed to have a swimming pool.

We topped a gentle rise and a hundred yards ahead of us was a dog, a short-legged black and tan dog with a familiar rolling gait. A basset, trotting up the road. Barbara exclaimed, "Penny!"

I slowed the car. The dog turned off the road at a rural mailbox, went up a driveway to a gray Cape Cod house set a little way back, almost at the edge of the woodland. I braked to a stop at the head of the driveway and Barbara shouted, "Penny! Penny!"

The dog paid no attention.

"Drive in!"

"It's not Penny. It's an older dog."

"Please. I have to find out. You know as well as I do that if Penny decided to go somewhere, Sybil couldn't stop her. Please!"

I drove up the driveway. The dog had disappeared. Barbara went to the door and knocked. A woman in a turtleneck sweater and pink slacks answered.

"The basset that just came in here," Barbara asked. "It's Penny, isn't it?"

"The basset? Oh, did he just come home?"

"Yes. We followed her up the driveway, and—Oh, there she is! Penny!"

The dog came around the corner of the house, stopped and stared. The woman laughed. "Sorry, but it's a he. Lord Jeff, we call him." The dog went to her, glanced at Barbara in the rather distant way of the more supercilious bassets, then went past the woman and into the house.

"I'm sorry to have bothered you," Barbara said, and turned back toward the car.

"There *is* a basset named Penny, I believe," the woman said, "who gets around quite a bit." She said it with a knowing smile. "But I haven't seen her in some time."

"Thanks." And Barbara got into the car. I turned around and we went back to the highway. It was another six miles to Sybil's place. We didn't see another dog.

Sybil came to the door while we were parking. We were halfway up the path when she said, "You're going to hate me. I said I would keep her in, but she's gone."

"She's not here?"

Sybil laughed ruefully. "Come on in and sit down and

145

have a drink. That dog is just too bright for her own good. We can visit, and maybe she'll come back. You never know, with Penny."

We sat on the couch in the living room, as before. Sybil got drinks. "That dog!" she exclaimed as she sat down. "She knew I was keeping her in, but she pretended not to care one little bit. She waited and bided her time. She knew— I don't know how she knows these things, but she does— she knew Bob had to go to town today. So she just waited till he got his coat on and was all ready to go. Then she crept up behind him, and the minute he opened the door one crack, out she went. She almost knocked him over. I made a grab for her and got hold of her collar, but just with two fingers. She ripped off those two fingernails." She held up her right hand, with the two broken nails. "Out she went, like a streak. And then she didn't know where to go. She hung around for half an hour before she actually disappeared."

I lifted my glass. "To the free soul."

Barbara glanced at me with a faint smile. Sybil said, "I never knew a more completely blithe and free spirit. I think that's probably what makes her so appealing." She stood up. "You haven't seen her in a long time. I've got some pictures."

She left the room, came back with an album of snapshots, handed the album to us and stood there as we leafed through.

"She's grown up, as you can see. Lost the puppy look. Oh, she's a very handsome dog now. But you can see that independent air, can't you? It's written all over her. . . . Oh, now in that picture she has the sedate look. But see that look in her eyes, the way her ears set? She's all ready to tell you right where you can go. You can go your way, she's about to tell you, and I'll go mine. . . . I wonder. I just thought, maybe she's down at Marion's. Marion lives not far from the ski lodge, and Penny goes to visit her every week or so. Marion feeds her steak and lets her sleep on her best sofa. I'll just give Marion a call, if you'll excuse me a minute." She went into another room.

"Want to bet?" I asked Barbara.

"On what?"

"That Penny's at Marion's."

"I wouldn't bet a penny on anything about her."

"She knew we were coming. She thought we were coming to get her. That's why she took off."

"How did she know?"

"She heard Sybil tell Bob."

"Then why did she go to Marion's?"

"For a steak dinner."

"She should have known that Marion would turn her in."

"That's why she didn't stay. She's not at Marion's. Want to bet?"

Sybil came back, shaking her head. "Wouldn't you know it? Penny was there. She had lunch with Marion, then took a short nap on that sofa. She woke up just about half an hour ago and wanted out, and Marion hasn't seen her since."

Barbara and I looked at each other, and she smiled. "Half an hour ago," she said, "just about the time we arrived."

"Maybe she's on her way home," Sybil said. But there wasn't any conviction in her voice. "She should be here by now. When she starts anywhere, she doesn't dawdle."

She went to the window and looked out, turned back shaking her head. "No sign of her yet. When she comes she'll bark and let me know she's here. Night or day, she barks when she comes home." She sat down again. "Did I tell you she's got a charge account at the butcher's, down in the village? Last spring she took to going in there and begging for a bone. The butcher told me, so I said just let her have what she wants and send us a bill. He hasn't billed me yet for steak or calves' liver, but he has sent a bill for several bones.

"And," she went on, "she learned to sing. She never sang for you, did she? Well, my dogs sing. They actually do. In the morning, usually, before I get up. Not howling, but— well, singing is the only word I can think of for it. A kind of warbling, and they each have a different part, tenor, alto, soprano. It really is quite musical, but thank goodness they never do it in the middle of the night. Well, anyway, Penny never joined them and I thought she wouldn't ever sing. Then one morning a few months ago when they started to sing I heard a new voice chime in. A good voice, very good. Baritone. I couldn't believe it, but it was Penny, sure enough. She doesn't always sing when the other dogs do, but when she does she makes it rather special. . . . She should be here by now. If she's coming."

"Maybe she went the other way."

"You never can tell about her. She has her own way of doing things. I should have put the leash on her this morning, but if I chain her up she's absolutely miserable. She just sits and looks at you. She makes you feel like a jailer. Then she whines and breaks your heart."

148

Barbara got to her feet. "We really should be going along."

"I know you can't spend the day. And I can't tell you how sorry I am that she isn't here. Maybe I should have phoned, but I kept thinking she would come home. . . . I know you have to go. But I keep hoping she'll come back and you can see her. . . . So many things I keep wanting to tell you. You said she used to snap at children. Up here she stays longest at places where they have kids. Little kids. . . . This will give you a laugh. We bought her a bed, one of those fancy wicker things with a hood and a mattress. Would she sleep in it? No, sir! Finally we put one of Bob's old Army blankets in a corner of the kitchen, and that's her bed now. She messes it around and won't let another dog near it. . . . Well, I guess she's not coming. But believe me, she's a magnificent dog. I appreciate her. But you don't dare let yourself get attached to a dog like that. When she goes off, you never know if she'll ever come back or what will happen to her. And as I said, she's a loner. She doesn't travel with other dogs. I guess she doesn't need other dogs—or people, for that matter. Not permanently, anyway. So I just admire her and let her go her own way."

She went out to the car with us, watching the driveway for a dog that didn't arrive. We said good-bye. But when we reached the road Barbara said, "Let's go down the road a way, just to see if we meet her."

So we went down the road instead of going directly home. Not a dog in sight. We kept going till we came to the ski lodge and the slopes, deserted and waiting for snow. We pulled into the parking yard and looked around on foot. No dog.

149

We went on to the crossroads in the village, and turned around and started back. No use going any farther. We went back past the ski lodge, up the hills to the plateau, past Sybil's entrance. No sign of a basset anywhere. We had seen a couple of brindled hounds in the village, and there was an Irish setter in the dooryard of one of the houses we passed. That was the sum of it.

We drove on in the lengthening light of late afternoon, and Barbara said, "Well, now we know."

"What do we know?"

"That it wasn't our fault. Or Tom's and Carol's. She just isn't anybody's dog."

"Or maybe she's everybody's dog."

"She's at home anywhere, apparently."

"And expects to be treated like visiting royalty."

"Is treated that way. . . . I do wish we had seen her."

"You saw the pictures, and you heard Sybil's stories. It was almost a memorial service. I kept listening for 'Abide with Me' on the organ offstage."

"You're just talking tough, and you know it. You were disappointed too at not seeing her."

"I hid my tears pretty well, didn't I?"

She didn't answer. We drove in silence another five or six miles. Then in a field off to the right I saw a dog, or what I thought was a black and tan dog. It was so far away and the grass was so high I couldn't see any details, and the light made colors deceiving. It was an animal, and it was crossing the field diagonally toward the edge of the far hill. I lifted a hand and pointed, and I slowed the car. Barbara looked and exclaimed, "A fox! A red fox!" I looked again. Maybe she was right, though I couldn't see the bushy tail with its white tip. But it was a long way off, two hundred yards or more.

We drove on, and I asked, "Do you want to stop in Barrington and have supper?"

"Let's go on home and just—well, be glad we went. We had to know."

"We still don't know. I don't."

"We know that chapter, anyway. Enough. That rounds it out for me. But I do wonder how it will end."

We went home, thinking the Penny story was closed, regardless of how it might end for Sybil.

Two weeks later Sybil called. Barbara took the call, then came back to the living room and said, "Sybil. Penny's gone."

"Again?"

"Yet. She never did come back. Sybil hasn't seen her since that morning when she bolted out the door, the day we went up there. Nobody else has seen her, since she had lunch at Marion's. She simply dropped out of sight."

"What does Sybil think?"

"She doesn't know what to think."

"Was she upset?"

"No. Hurt, more than anything else."

"Well, that *was* a nice memorial service."

Barbara sat silent, looking at the fire. "What *do* you suppose happened, anyway? Did she hitch a ride with someone going to Florida? Or Arizona? Did she light out and just keep going? Did she get hit by a car or a truck and crawl off into the brush and die?"

"Not that," I said. "If Penny got hurt she would demand an ambulance and a nurse and an intern—and get them! And a private room in the hospital."

"All right. Have it your way. Suppose you tell me just what is your version of what happened. And when you get through, I'll tell you my version."

So we spent the whole evening telling each other what happened to Penny.

Thirteen ❧

Abby, I said, starting my version of the story, was suspiciously friendly that morning. Penny had not even had breakfast when Abby came over to her and said, "We're going to miss you, darling. We'll miss you terribly."

Penny knew that tone. She sniffed. "I can't truthfully say I wish I could say as much."

Abby smiled, that smirk which was little more than a

deepening of her age lines. "Penny, dear, you needn't try to tell us. We know how you feel. But maybe those friends of yours with that great big estate and all those servants will let you come and visit us once in a while. Then you can tell us more of your tall tales about life among the grandees."

Sybil was setting out Penny's breakfast. "Big-ear Abby," Penny said under her breath. "You can hear a bit of gossip a mile off, can't you? How would you like to have one of those big ears chewed off?"

"Oh, darling! Touchy this morning, aren't you?" Abby showed her old, worn teeth in a false smile. Then she asked, "They are coming, aren't they?"

Penny turned to the dish of canned dog food. She didn't really like it, but she always ate the morning meal because she never knew what the rest of the day would bring.

"They're coming today, aren't they?" Abby persisted.

"Oh, go scratch your fleas!" Penny snapped. "What business is it of yours, anyway?"

Sybil heard them but didn't understand what they were saying. "Abby," she ordered, "go away and let Penny alone. You've had your breakfast."

Abby went back to the other dogs and whispered something at which they all laughed. But they left Penny alone, and when she had finished eating she went to her blanket, licked her face clean and pretended to doze while Sybil took up breakfast for Bob. She called him and he came, dressed for town, smelling of shaving lotion. They ate in the alcove and Penny could hear every word they said. Most of it was unimportant, but Penny caught things like, "They said they would be here around two-thirty. . . . No, I don't think they

154

will want to take her. They just want to see her. But if they should want her back . . . well, she never has really settled down here. . . . She loves it here, Bob. It's just that—Yes, I know. She's a 'free soul.' . . . Well, she is. Are you sure you can't be back by then? I'd like you to meet them. . . . I'll see."

Then they had finished breakfast. Penny knew the routine on going-to-town days. He would go upstairs, be gone five minutes, come back with his coat on, say, "Well, I'll get going," glance at the dogs, say "Good-bye, dogs." They would yelp at him, in chorus, Abby leading. The expected response. He would go to the door, open it, turn to kiss Sybil and leave.

Penny stood up, stretched casually, eased over toward the door. Bob came downstairs, and Abby began to yelp almost before he gave the signal. He laughed and went to the door, unlatched it, turned to kiss Sybil. And Penny made her dash. The door was open a crack. She struck it with her shoulder, pushed, pushed it full open, almost upset Bob and was outside, free.

There was loud talk and a chorus of barking inside. Bob came out and shouted, "Penny! Come back here, Penny!"

Penny moved toward the garage, to have room to maneuver. Sybil came out, trying to hide the leash in her hand. "Come, Penny," she urged, soothing. "Come on, like a good dog. Come, Penny."

Penny debated a moment. Some days she let them think they could catch her and kept them cajoling and threatening for half an hour. She decided not to play that game today. If Big-mouth Abby had kept quiet, she might have, but she wasn't feeling playful now. She wanted to get away from them, all of them. She turned and trotted down the driveway toward the road.

She was almost at the gateway when she heard Bob's car coming. She turned aside into the bushes, just in case he decided to stop and try to collar her. But he didn't stop. Penny went back to the driveway, followed him a moment, then turned and went the opposite direction. There wasn't much action in that direction. She knew that. But she refused to follow Bob's car, just on general principles.

There was one place up the road a few miles where she usually was welcome. She didn't often go there because they had a cat she didn't like, one of those big, hairy Persian things that put on airs and tried to make Penny feel like a scrounger. The last time she was there Penny got so fed up with that cat's insolence that she chased her up a tree. The woman called Penny a very bad-mannered dog and said she wouldn't be welcome there if she didn't mend her ways. But maybe she had forgotten by now. No harm just stopping by, to see.

She trotted up the road, in no hurry at all. The day was young. She wondered how her Connecticut People, as she still called them, were by now. All right, so she had told some fancy stories about life with them on the farm. It had been fun most of the time. She wondered if the cows were still there—vicious, dog-killing bulls, in her stories. And the highway trucks, prehistoric monsters. And the sweeper, a fearful dog-eating dragon. None of the other dogs had ever seen a dog-eating dragon, let alone challenging it, stopping it in its tracks.

They were due about two-thirty, Sybil had said. They

would be on time. They were punctual. He had always put
Penny to bed at eight-thirty, got her up at five-thirty, on the
dot. Gruff, but pleasant enough if you did things his way.
Made quite a fuss if you didn't. As for Her, she was softhearted, thought Penny was a dear. Most of the time. . . .
Well, she might go back and look them over. Or she might
not, depending on what the day brought.

A big truck came roaring down the road, and she moved
over onto the grassy shoulder to be well out of its way. A
bird was there, a long-billed flicker working an anthill. When
the big truck whooshed past, the rush of air blew the flicker
right off the ground. It almost knocked Penny over. The bird
fluttered in the air, caught itself and flew away. Penny
trotted on, telling herself a brand new story about the prehistoric monster that could blow an eagle into the air with
one puff of its breath.

She came in sight of the house with the big, hairy cat and
left the road to take a shortcut. As she crawled through a
fence her license tag was snagged in a loop of wire. Brought
up short, she braced her legs, hauled back and jammed the
tag still tighter. She tossed her head from side to side,
braced all four legs and jerked. The brass tag was worn thin
at the top, from all her jingling travel. It gave way, ripped
loose from the link to her collar. She was free. And, in a legal
sense, she was anonymous, an untagged dog.

The incident annoyed her, but only briefly. She crossed
the field to the house. No one was there, not even the cat.
The house was closed and shuttered. But instead of going
back to the highway at once she crossed the field back of
the house, came to the woodland, put up a rabbit and had a
good run. Finally the rabbit ran in at an old stone wall and

Penny, after sniffing the wonderful smells—the wall had been haven for many rabbits, a skunk or two, a fox and several raccoons—turned back. Hot from the chase, she wanted a drink. There was a brook near the house with the big, hairy cat. She went back there, drank, rested in the shade. Then she decided to go see Marion.

It was getting toward noon when she arrived at Marion's house, a good time to get there. She went to the kitchen door and barked politely. She was always the lady with Marion. Marion answered her bark, invited her in, rubbed her ears, said sweet nothings and told her to go lie down on the big, soft sofa till lunch was ready. And when lunch was ready Marion dished up a special plate for Penny. Not steak, but some kind of stew. Penny ate it, ladylike, not spattering one drop on the floor, and licked her chops and thanked Marion with her eyes. Then she went back to the sofa and went to sleep. She dreamed about her Connecticut People and wakened with a start. It was almost time for them to arrive at Sybil's. But she didn't leap down and dash to the door. She yawned and stretched and made it all seem very casual. But when Marion let her out she headed for the shortcut.

She hadn't taken the shortcut in months. It led across an old pasture and through a woodland, past a farm with two hounds, one old and grumpy, the other young and rather handsome. The last time she went that way the old hound had threatened to tear her to bits, and both of them had chased her. She had run, but just enough to make them feel important: then she had let them catch up and learn that she was a girl. She didn't often use her sex to put a dog in his place, but there were occasions when a touch of femininity came in handy.

158

As she crossed the field and went through the woodland she wondered if those hounds were still there. The young one, she remembered, had something—well, something that made her remember. She came to the farm and, as before, the hounds came charging out of the dooryard. And as before, she let them chase her a little way, then catch up. The old one was grizzled about the muzzle and stiff in the hocks, but the young one was even better looking than she remembered. He was all apologies. "Haven't I seen you before?" he asked. One of that kind. But she played his game. He nosed her and rubbed shoulders and danced around, and when she went on he accompanied her. The old hound grumbled, "Wasting your time on a nobody, a little bitch that came out of the woods." But the young hound called him "an envious old has-been pooch" and strutted like a show dog. The two of them, Penny and the young hound— "Just call me Mack, darling"—went down the lane together.

Penny forgot all about her people from Connecticut. She pretended that she picked up a rabbit scent and went dashing off across a pasture, just to see if Mack would follow. He did. Then he pretended that he had a fox scent. She followed him. But he outdistanced her so far he had to have his imaginary fox circle back past her to give her a chance to catch him. They rolled in the grass. They nipped each other's ears. They yelped at each other. They chased each other into an old sheep pasture with a winding road at the foot of the hill. Mack became more and more insistent. Penny dodged and twisted and scrambled down the gravelly hillside. Mack, trying to turn and follow her, lost his footing, rolled into a clump of hardhack and was twenty yards behind when Penny darted through the hedgerow onto the

159

winding blacktop road. She was looking back, watching for Mack, and didn't hear or see the low white car with red racing stripes.

Brakes squealed. Tires skidded. A girl screamed, "There's a dog!" Penny looked up just in time to see the black width of a tire and try to dodge. She didn't quite make it, but instead of being hit squarely and crushed like a bug under a thumb she got a glancing blow that caved in her ribs and knocked her into the roadside grass. The car came to a stop fifty yards beyond and a blonde girl leaped out, came running back, a young man right behind her. The girl knelt beside Penny, whispered, "Oh, you poor darling," and began to cry.

The man asked, "Dead?"

The girl shook her head. "Very badly hurt, though. See those poor ribs? She's barely breathing." Very gently, she picked Penny up in her arms.

The young man looked at Penny's collar, shook his head. "No tag. She doesn't belong to anyone. Just a stray."

"I don't believe it!" the girl exclaimed. "It's an expensive collar. Besides, she's a beautiful dog. Somebody loves her. She has a home."

"So what do we do now?"

"Take her to a vet. Or to a hospital. Somewhere where they will take care of her."

They carried Penny back to the car and the girl held her in her lap as they drove on. Penny drifted off into her own dreams.

She had been hurrying back to Sybil's, to meet her people from Connecticut. Being careful, as she always was, watching and listening for cars and trucks. And suddenly, out of nowhere, this great big fearful monster, a monster that could blow an eagle right out of the air with one breath, appeared and swished its tail at her as it passed. And just like that, with one swish of its tail, she was knocked clear off the road, fearfully hurt.

Then the ambulance had come, the big white ambulance, and a beautiful young blonde nurse named Gloria and a taciturn young intern named Dr. Fairfield. They put her on the stretcher and the nurse held Penny's paw and smoothed her forehead with her cool hand. The intern checked her heart with his stethoscope and said, "Plasma. She needs plasma," and he inserted the needle, connected the tubing, hung the bottle of plasma on the hook. Gloria said Penny's pulse was fluttery, so the intern gave her an injection.

Gloria said, "I wish we knew who she is. But there's not a scrap of identification. What is your name, dear? Can you hear me?"

Penny tried to rouse from the merciful coma but couldn't speak.

"Try hard, darling. Tell me your name."

Penny finally managed to whisper, "Penny . . . royal . . . prin—"

"Pennyroyal!" Gloria exclaimed. "Not the Princess Pennyroyal!"

Penny nodded slightly, but even that movement hurt dreadfully.

"Dr. Fairfield," Gloria said to the intern in an awed voice, "this is the Princess Pennyroyal!"

"Not—not the— Are you *sure?*"

161

"Positive. Haven't you seen her picture? I have, in *Life* and *Time* and *Newsweek*. And she just told me! Oh, Dr. Fairfield, we *must* save her!"

Dr. Fairfield gave Penny two more injections, then told the driver of the ambulance, "Call the hospital and rally all hands. We have Princess Pennyroyal with internal injuries and in an advanced state of shock from a car accident!" There was a series of squawks and squeals from the closed-circuit radio. The driver increased his speed to 60, 70, then 80 miles an hour. His siren screamed. Penny twitched, tried to howl, had to be quieted by Gloria's gentle, loving hands.

The nurses and two interns were waiting at the emergency entrance. They slid the stretcher out of the ambulance and in no time they were in the elevator, on the way up to the operating room. Dr. Bornemann and Dr. Smith had been waiting at the elevator. Dr. Bornemann held his stethoscope to her chest, listened intently. Dr. Smith took her pulse, nodded to Dr. Bornemann, who nodded in answer.

Out of the elevator, into the operating room. Dr. Lovallo was there, in his green suit. "How is her heart?" he asked Dr. Bornemann, still listening to his stethoscope. Dr. Bornemann nodded slowly, gravely. "Shall we operate?" Dr. Lovallo asked.

Dr. Smith said, "Operate, or she'll die like a dog." His voice was gruff with emotion.

Penny rallied and swam momentarily into consciousness. Lights everywhere, blinding lights overhead. Nurses and doctors around her, in green robes, all with masks over their mouths. "Please," Penny whispered, and everyone in the room was instantly silent. "If I should not survive—" One of the nurses began to sob, quickly stifled it. "If," Penny went

162

on, "I am unable to respond to your best efforts, please notify my family."

"Yes!" said Dr. Smith, bending close. "Yes! What address?"

"Just—just The Farm. My family on the farm—" Penny's voice faded away and she lapsed into unconsciousness again.

The anesthetist glanced at Dr. Lovallo, who nodded. The needle was inserted, the mask adjusted. A few minutes later Dr. Lovallo said, "The scalpel, please," and began the operation.

It was a long and difficult operation, but at last all the doctors agreed that everything possible had been done. They sighed and looked solemn, and one of them said, "Now it is out of our hands." Penny was taken to the recovery room, and from there to the private room.

It was a big corner room known as the Queen's Room. There Penny swam up through the mists and was vaguely aware of her surroundings. The room was warm, airy, full of sweet scents. The big windowsill was banked with flowers. Two nurses were there, a floor nurse named Diane and a private nurse named Rose.

"Well," Diane said, "we are waking up, are we?"

And Rose said, "We are very glad to see you, your Highness."

Diane brought a glass of cool water, with a sipper. Rose brought a cool, damp washcloth and gently washed her face. Word spread that Penny was awake, and others came: Alma with her gentle smile, Nancy to see that everything possible was done to make her comfortable. Penny had a dreadful headache and there was nothing in her abdomen but a huge, throbbing mass of pain. It hurt to breathe. Diane saw her wince and immediately gave her an injection.

Dusk came, and darkness. Dr. Lovallo appeared, now in a brown tweed suit, Dr. Bornemann in gray. They examined her, sent word for Dr. Smith. He came in, dapper in tweed jacket, weskit and slacks. They conferred.

"If she can hold on through the night," Dr. Smith finally said, "She has a chance."

Dr. Bornemann said, "It's touch and go."

And Dr. Lovallo said, "It could go either way."

Dr. Smith checked the intravenous needles and ordered another round when this one was gone. They stood at the bedside, watching her and looking grave. Then they left.

She was fretful, briefly conscious from time to time. Diane had left and Patricia had come. Rose left and Elsie took her place. The night wore on, the lights low and the nurses hushed and hurrying from room to room in silence. Finally there were the first streaks of dawn.

Penny had slept without waking almost two hours. Now she roused with more clarity than she had had since the accident. "Nurse," she called, and Elsie was at her bedside. "Yes?"

"You have been very kind," Penny said. "Everyone has. Please tell them for me, when I am—"

"There, there, dear. You can tell them later."

"No," Penny said. "I am going away. I have had a good life, even though a brief one. Excitement, love, joy, the whole wonderful experience of living. I have lived!"

"Yes, dear. And you will go on—"

Penny's eyelids fluttered. Her throat choked and she caught a shallow breath. "Yes," she said, "I am going on . . . on . . . on . . ." Her voice faded. Her eyes closed. And the

164

last thing she heard was the muffled sobbing of Elsie, the nurse.

For a little while she seemed to be nowhere, floating in a vast blue infinity of sky. Not moving, just floating, but somehow going somewhere. She didn't know where, and she didn't know how, and it didn't matter in the least. There was no more pain, and there was nothing to trouble her in any way. Then she was aware of something under her, something soft as down, soft as the softest cushion she ever slept on. All around her was this softness, a gleaming kind of cloud that seemed to be carrying her somewhere. And there was a sense of peace, of a sunlit meadow with a quiet brook and butterflies. She fell asleep.

Later, how much later she did not know, she was crossing that meadow and the cushiony cloud was gone. The grass was soft underfoot. The brook water, when she paused there for a drink, was the sweetest, coolest, clearest water she ever saw. Then she followed a path to a big red farmhouse at the far side of the meadow, and as she came close she saw a man and two dogs sitting on the front steps. He was an old man, with white hair and a long white beard, and he looked very friendly. One dog was a big brown and white Saint Bernard. The other was a black and white hound who looked like a cross between a beagle and a foxhound.

Penny hesitated at the edge of the dooryard, but the man said, "Hello, Penny. We've been expecting you. Come on up and see us."

Penny wondered how he knew her name. But lots of people knew who she was. She liked his voice. She went closer and hesitated again.

The man held out his hand. "Come on," he urged. "We want to talk to you." And at last she went right up to him and he rubbed her ears and she licked his hand. "My name is Peter," he said. "And these are my two special assistants for canine affairs. This big fellow is Saint Bernard, whom you may have heard of. And this young strutter," he said with a laugh as he turned to the black and white hound, "is—well, I *call* him Saint Pat. Not really a saint, but he deserves a title. Just call him Pat, if you like. . . . And now, young lady, account for yourself."

Penny hardly knew what to say, but she sensed that she must tell the truth, that Peter and his assistants would know if she told even the tiniest falsehood. So she told them the truth, or a reasonable approximation, with only a few tall tales thrown in. Peter shook a finger at her once, and Saint Bernard huffed once, but Saint Pat just sat there and smiled when she called the road sweeper a prehistoric dog-eater. She decided she liked Saint Pat best of all of them.

She told her story, and Peter turned to Saint Bernard and asked, "Well, what do you think?" And Saint Bernard nodded and looked very solemn, though there was a twinkle in his eyes. "You?" Peter asked Saint Pat.

Pat actually smiled. "She stays, or I go," he said.

And Peter leaned back and laughed and slapped his knee, and then leaned forward and rubbed Penny's ears. "All right, honey, you stay." Then he turned to Saint Pat. "And since you come from the same county down there"—and he pointed with his finger—"why don't you show Miss Penny around? Catch up on gossip about the home folks too."

And Saint Pat, who preferred to be known as just plain Pat, said, "Thank you, Peter. I'll be honored to do just that."

Pat and Penny started down the walk from the red farm-house together, just like old, old friends, and Peter shouted, "You needn't hurry back. We'll have cook save supper for you. Both of you."

And they trotted off across the pasture toward the woods and the mountainside where Pat had run the rabbits ten years before Penny was born. They seemed to be having as good a time as though they were in dog heaven.

Fourteen ⌁

Penny, Barbara said, starting her version of the story, was as good as pie that morning. She didn't quarrel with the other dogs or disturb the cat or spill her breakfast on the floor. She had resolved to be a new dog, get along with everybody, love the world and do what was asked of her. She made that resolution every third day, and sometimes in between. But this morning she also resolved to do things the way *they* wanted them done.

And then, when he came down to breakfast, Bob said to her, "Penny, I want you to stay home today. Understand? No rambling off to see who will give you the best free meal in the county." He smiled when he said it, but Penny knew that tone in his voice. It made her bristle inside and automatically say to herself, "I won't. You can't make me."

Sybil said, "She's a very good dog, aren't you, Penny? And she's going to stay home until the people from Connecticut come." Penny knew that voice, too. Why was it that women who wanted you to do things their way had to treat you like a moron? Look you right in the eye and call you "She," as though you were somebody else and didn't know it.

But she thought, All right, I'll do it their way this time. And she was still in that frame of mind when Bob came downstairs with his coat on, ready to go. He went to the door, held it ajar as usual and turned to Sybil. Sybil said, "Wait just a sec, till I get a leash on her," and went to the closet. That did it. If doing things their way today meant being on a leash, she wanted none of it. She made a dash for the door, almost knocked Bob down and was outside before Sybil even reached the closet.

She didn't wait to see what happened next. She took to the brushy hillside back of the barn. She did hear Sybil calling her once or twice, and then she heard Bob's car drive off. She went on up the hill.

Well, so much for good resolutions. Again. Something always happened. Sybil said she admired Penny's free spirit, and then what did she do? Try to curb it. What was so

wonderful about sitting around all day on a leash, waiting
for somebody to come and say, "Why, hello Penny! Don't
you remember me?" And then talk about all the crazy, child-
ish things Penny did once. What was so wonderful about
waiting for anything, period? For the next meal. For a kind
word. For tomorrow. Yesterday and tomorrow could take
care of themselves. Anybody could have them. Today was
what counted.

She went over the brushy hilltop and cut back to the road.
The school bus was coming. It would stop at the next driveway. She ran and got there just in time. A little girl and a
little boy named Jane and Dick got on, and then Penny got
on. The driver waited for her, closed the door and all the
children shouted, "Hello, Penny!" Two little boys tried to
pull her ears and two little girls pushed them away and said,
"Nice Penny, come and sit with us." Which she did.

One of the little girls opened her lunch box and gave
Penny a coconut cookie. Penny didn't like coconut so she
slobbered most of the cookie onto the floor, and the driver
looked back and said, "Clean that up, you kids, and don't
feed the dog. Understand? This is a school bus, not a pigpen."

One little boy shouted, "Pigpen, pigpen, Penny's in a
pigpen." Others took up the chant. Everybody joined in,
even Penny, until the driver threatened to turn around and
take them all home if they didn't shut up.

They were still chanting when they reached the school.
Everybody got off. Penny went inside and visited several
rooms, debating; then she decided this wasn't a schoolday
for her. School wasn't like the ski lodge, anyway. Nobody
fed her salami sandwiches. All they ever gave her were

170

coconut cookies and peanut butter sandwiches. Peanut butter, ugh! She almost gagged at the memory of how it stuck in her mouth. As bad as bubble gum.

The bell rang and the hallways were crowded, so she waited till all were in their rooms and then she left. She went down to the village main street. She said good morning to the butcher, and he called her Bad Penny and said "Back again" and laughed at her. But he gave her a scrap of the boiled ham he was getting ready to slice. "On the house," he said. Penny didn't really like ham, but it took the coconut taste away.

She went on down the street, said good morning to the postmaster and the grocer and the hardware man. She met two of the village dogs, fat old house dogs, and she wandered about with them for a time, listening to their talk about the good old days. To hear them tell it, there hadn't been anything worth seeing or doing since they were puppies, eight or ten years ago. Penny preened and strutted, but they were so busy reminiscing that they scarcely saw her. She called them a pair of old fuddy-duddies and left them. She decided there wasn't much excitement in the village today and began to wonder what Marion was having for lunch. It was still early, but she started to Marion's house, taking the shortcut through the woods. There she found a fresh rabbit scent and spent an hour running the rabbit in big circles and then sniffing and whining at the stone wall where it ran in. By then she was less than half a mile from Marion's house.

Marion answered her first bark and gave her the usual welcome. Marion asked her about Sybil and Abby and the other dogs. The house smelled of cooking, something with herbs in it. Penny didn't care for herbs. But she stayed, and pretty soon Marion said, "Lunchtime, Penny!" Penny was all set for a juicy piece of steak. But Marion began dishing up stew. She put it in the dish she always used for Penny and set it aside to cool. "Sorry, Penny," she said, "but there's not one bit of steak today. So you're going to have the same thing I do—savory beef stew. Ummm!" she said, and smacked her lips. "You'll love it!"

Penny didn't care for stew, savory or not. But it was better than nothing. She waited, and pretty soon Marion set it on the floor for her and Penny ate, slowly, carefully, pushing the chunk of carrot to the side of her dish instead of putting it on the floor. Marion sat at the kitchen table and ate her own stew, telling Penny again how very tasty it was, and she told Penny about the letters she had written that morning. Penny wasn't the least bit interested. She licked her chops clean and went into the living room and climbed up on the sofa and went to sleep.

She slept till almost two o'clock, then went to the door and Marion let her out. Not much of a day, Penny thought. Hardly worth the bother of running away this morning. First Bob, then Sybil, then— Oh, the children in the school bus were all right, but they were just kids. Then those two old dogs in the village, who wouldn't give her a leer, not even a second look. And stew instead of steak. She belched the herbs and made a face at the taste. Well, she might as well go back and see the Connecticut People. It was only a few miles, and at least they would be different faces, different voices. She turned up the road toward Sybil's place.

She hadn't gone a mile when a dark green panel truck drew up beside her, a truck she had never seen before. A man with a walrus mustache leaned out and said, "Hello, Spot. Aren't you a real dandy, though!"

Penny stopped and looked at him. He had a pleasant enough voice. The man beside him, a man with a blond beard, said, "Not a car nor a house in sight. All's clear!" And the first man opened the door and said, "Come on, hop in, Spot."

Penny decided maybe he was another mailman or bus driver. She welcomed a ride. She scrambled in and the man with the beard had her by the collar before the door was shut. "Hmmm!" he said. "Real class. Probably pedigreed. She must have cost a pretty penny."

The other man, the driver, said, "Probably worth more at a kennel than she is at the lab."

The man holding Penny took a pair of nippers from his pocket, snipped her license tag from her collar and threw it into the roadside ditch. "There," he said. "Now you're just a dog, anybody's dog. A pretty-penny dog." And Penny rather liked him. He knew her name. She tried to put her paws on the window ledge, to see where they were going, but he said, "No, you don't, Fido! You stay right here till you go in back with the rest of them."

They passed Sybil's driveway and kept on going. They drove another hour before they turned off onto a side road, then onto a track that led into a woodland. There they parked and the men got out, the one with the beard still holding Penny in his arms. They went to the back of the truck, unlocked and opened the door. Inside was a heavy mesh cage with four dogs in it, all asleep. One, an English setter, opened one eye and tried to lift its head but seemed

173

to lack the strength. A strange sweetish odor came from the cage.

The driver filled a hypodermic needle from a bottle in his pocket and asked, "Ready?"

The man holding Penny said, "Shoot," and reached for Penny's collar.

Before he got hold of the collar, the driver ruffled the hair on Penny's hip and jabbed with the needle. Penny yelped with pain and surprise, made a convulsive leap and was out of the bearded man's arms. She struck the ground running. The men cursed and shouted, then ran after her. She scurried through the brush, running for her life.

She soon outdistanced them in the tangled underbrush. But suddenly her legs felt very tired. She had to slow to a walk. Instinct told her to find a hiding place. She crawled into a clump of bushes, found a deep bed of leaves, wallowed into it, quivering, not knowing what had happened. Five minutes and she was asleep, drugged by about two thirds of the dose of sedative the man had tried to inject. The rest of it squirted into the air as she leaped free. But that partial dose had now taken effect.

She slept hidden there in the bushes the rest of the afternoon and into the night, wakened wondering where she was and aware only of a dizzying headache. She slept again, till daylight, and wakened enough to stagger to her feet. Her tongue was thick and she was parched. She found a path and followed it to a sweet-smelling brook, where she drank her fill. Then she lay in the water and cooled her whole body. Some of the confusion cleared, but only enough so that she knew she must keep going. She went all that day, keeping to the woods and fields. She slept in the brush again that night, and the next morning was so hungry she went into a village looking for a school or a butcher shop. She was hungry enough to welcome peanut butter sandwiches or ham.

She was still bleary-eyed and her legs were wobbly. Before she found either school or butcher shop she came to a filling station, and just then an old scarred bus rolled up and stopped across the street. It looked as though it had come a long way, and there were several mattresses piled in a jumble on the back seats. A group of young people got out, all with long hair and in bare feet, most of them in dungarees. Two had beards and several had drooping mustaches. The others probably were girls. Obviously a girl was the only one in a dress, a long, gypsy-skirted green and yellow dress. They all came across the street to the rest rooms and Penny went over to the bus, sniffed, didn't smell food and reluctantly turned away.

By then the first of them were coming back. The girl in the gypsy dress saw Penny and cried, "Look! A dog!"

One of the men shouted, "Steal this dog!"

The girl said, "Hello, Doggykins. Want to join the commune?" Her voice was friendly. Penny tried to go to her, staggered, almost fell. "Wow!" the girl exclaimed. "She's stoned!"

"One of us," someone said with a laugh, and the girl picked Penny up in her arms and carried her into the bus.

They all came back and the bus went on. A little way and the girl with Penny in her arms said, "I'm starved. So is Doggykins."

"Soul food," someone said. "Eat the soul food."

But the girl said, "I need some body food. Get me some sweet rolls."

175

The driver stopped at a store, the girl gave another girl a few nickels and dimes, and she brought back a plastic bagful of sweet buns. A tall, thin blond young man clad only in stagged-off dungarees chanted, "One a penny, two a penny, hot cross buns, If you have no daughters, feed them to your dog." And Penny wondered how they knew her name.

They drove on, and the girl fed Penny all the sweet buns she could eat. She liked the sweetness, but the doughiness was hard to swallow. She needed something in her stomach, though. When she had stuffed herself, she went to the back of the bus and crawled up on a mattress. She slept most of the day, while the bus rattled and wheezed down the road. From time to time someone strummed a guitar and sang a monotonous song about how far it was from anywhere and how little anything mattered.

Late afternoon and Penny wakened just as they were crossing a big river on a high bridge. Some of the dizziness was gone, but she still staggered when she tried to walk down the aisle of the lurching bus. Everybody laughed at her and somebody offered her a drink of beer. She didn't like it. She found the girl in the long dress, whom the others called Liz. Liz found a jug of water and poured some for her in a tin cup.

They came to a shopping center and parked, and Liz and one of the other girls and one of the boys went into a big supermarket. When they came back Liz had a paper bag with a carton of milk and half a dozen oranges.

"Operation complete?" the driver asked.

Liz nodded. "We ripped them. Let's go."

The bus wheeled out of the yard and down the street. Out

176

of town, the driver pulled into a side road that led down to an old meadow beside a brook. He parked and Liz began taking things out of her long, voluminous dress—three big beefsteaks, half a dozen packets of cold cuts, a frozen pizza, a dressed chicken, two bags of potato chips, olives, pickles, a long loaf of French bread.

That night they camped there and cooked over an open fire. Penny had her beefsteak, and the next morning she had almost completely recovered. Enough, at least, to hear them talk about Georgia and Carolina and the various camps and communes they were going to visit. But also enough to be aware for the first time of what was making her feel queasy every time she walked down the aisle of the bus. It was the smell. Not only a lived-in, people smell, but the smell of dirty feet, bare dirty feet. She decided to stay up on a seat as much as she could.

They went on, mostly southward but varying the route from day to day, going pretty much where whim suggested, never going more than two hundred miles a day. And every day Liz and one of the other girls went into a supermarket while the others waited in the bus and came back with an assortment of food that had been liberated, as they said. You never knew what was going to happen next, where they would go, what they would eat. And nobody told Penny what to do. For the first few days she thought it was just the life she had been yearning for. Then she began to wonder why nobody cared what she did, or what anybody did. Something was missing, though she didn't know what.

She hadn't found the answer when Liz got into trouble. They had parked at a supermarket and Liz and the girl called Marg had gone in. Five minutes later Marg came running out. The man at the wheel of the bus saw her coming, started the motor and was on his way out of the yard when she caught up and leaped aboard. "They got Liz!" she gasped, and the driver roared away and down the street, around two corners and down a back alley. They got away, out of town, leaving Liz behind. But at the next town the police flagged them down and took them off to jail. Penny didn't wait to see what happened next. Off the bus, she was on her own again.

She went on, scrounging as she went, finding a scrap in a garbage can, begging a part of a hamburger at a drive-in, finding a dish of partly eaten dog food on someone's back step, sleeping wherever night found her.

One evening she came to a town with a carnival, and she was drawn to the sounds of gaiety and the bright lights. She wandered down the midway, wary and wily. A youngster dropped a wad of cotton candy, and Penny thrust her tongue at it, found it a puff of sweet nothing. A small boy with a hot dog in his hand stood gaping at the merry-go-round, and Penny snatched the hot dog, bun and all, and ran. She thought she heard her name and went to the booth where they were pitching coins at a dish on a table. "Right this way!" the barker called. "Pitch 'em high or pitch 'em low! Pitch a lucky penny and win a dollar. Penny, penny, penny! Come and pitch a penny." She waited, but nobody she knew was there, and nobody seemed to know her. She went back to the merry-go-round, where the music was a tune that Herb Alpert played, when she was with her people on the farm in Connecticut. Nobody she knew there, either. She turned, and across the way was the fat lady in the side show. She was trying to sell photographs of herself in odd and unusual poses, and had no customers. Then she saw Penny and she called, "Well, Doggy-woggy! Come to Mamma. Oh, you little darling, you!" Penny stood and stared, and the fat lady began to chuckle, a chuckle that shook her tiered chins and her bulging belly. "What *are* you thinking? A penny for your thoughts?" Penny had two thoughts. One, How did she know my name? Two, People pick dogs that look like them. Do I look like that?

She turned and ran.

Then one day she came to a trailer court. The cars and their trailers seemed to have the smell of adventure, yet the smell of home too. She went down the line and stopped at a big trailer, gleaming and scrubbed and looking luxurious. It had a side canopy, and a woman was sitting in the shade on a folding chair, reading a book. Penny went close, and the woman looked up and said, "Hello, stranger. Whose dog are you?" Penny wagged her tail and would have lain down beside her chair if she had been invited. But the woman went back to her book and Penny went on. She had learned that people who spoke that way were merely being polite.

She came to a medium-size trailer where a man was oiling a pair of leather boots. He had an outdoors look and a smell of dog, even from ten feet away. Penny stopped and he looked up and saw her and exclaimed, "Well, hello, sweetheart!"

There was a sound inside the trailer and a woman appeared at the door, a woman with blonde hair and wearing a tight sweater and tight slacks. "Yeah?" she said, and the man looked at her and laughed.

"You don't miss a trick, do you? Well, look at this!" He pointed to Penny. "Look at this sweetheart."

The woman looked and said, "Another dog."

He held out his hand and Penny went to him. He rubbed her head, felt her shoulders. "A damn fine basset, Louise. And no license."

The woman shook her head. "You need another dog like you need another hole in your head. Two dogs at home and four at the camp."

He still fondled Penny's ear. "But, Sweetie—"

She cut him short with a laugh. "Of course, if you want *another* bitch—"

And he said, "You win," and turned to Penny. "Sorry, babe, but I've got a full house."

Penny knew the tone. Dismissal. She went on down the line, glancing at each trailer.

Then a boy about ten years old saw her and called, "Here, dog, here, dog!" He had longish, sun-faded reddish hair, freckles on his cheeks, and he was skinny as a willow stick. He wore only faded jeans stagged off short and raveling into an uneven fringe. He toes wriggled as he talked. Penny liked him at first sight. She went to him and he squatted down and held her, one ear in each fist, and looked her in the eyes. "My name's Rusty. What's yours?" She thrust out her tongue and licked his nose and squirmed with pleasure. He exclaimed, "Slobbers!" and wiped his nose with his bare forearm, then leaped to his feet, shouted, "Come on, Slobbers!" and dashed off.

Penny ran after him. He led the way to the last trailer on the line, a medium-size one that could do with a bit of polish and looked comfortably lived in. He went to the door and shouted, "Mom! Hey, Mom, I got a dog named Slobbers!"

Out of the trailer came a girl maybe two years older than Rusty, also in stagged-off jeans but with a man-size white T shirt on. After her came another boy of perhaps six, in bathing trunks too big for him. Then a little girl of perhaps three, in nothing but white underpants. And after them all came a woman dressed exactly like the older girl, T shirt and all, but wearing blue sneakers. She was the only one not barefoot. She had short reddish hair and freckles like Rusty, and bright blue eyes like his. "Where," she demanded, "did you pick up that dog?"

"I didn't pick her up, Mom. She picked me! And look— no license tag! She isn't anybody's, so she belongs to me. Finders keepers!"

"Rusty," Mom said, in a warning tone.

"Honest, Mom. It's the truth. Absolutely. I was coming along, and here she comes, just like she's looking for me." He spread the fingers of one hand in a pleading gesture. "What could I do?"

The littlest one was hugging Penny, saying, "Doggy, doggy, doggy." Penny licked her face and she laughed.

The woman tightened her lips and checked a smile. But before she could say anything, Rusty said, "I can keep her, can't I, Mom? She won't eat much, I bet. She can have my breakfast. I don't like breakfast much anyway."

The older girl had squatted down, was rubbing Penny's ears. She looked up at Mom with Rusty's question in her eyes.

Mom hesitated, then said, "You'll have to ask— Oh, here he comes now."

A lean, dark-haired man came down the line, a spring in his walk, a grin on his face as he saw them all beside the

181

trailer. "Well," he said, "what's the convention about? To welcome me home?"

"Dad!" Rusty exclaimed.

"Dad," said the older girl.

"Bill," said the woman.

"Yes? . . . Ladies first, then girls, then the menfolk." He turned to Mom, then saw Penny and exclaimed, "Well, I'll be —! Where did that come from?"

"Rusty found her somewhere, he says, and she doesn't seem to have any license, so—"

"So we need a dog? This dog?"

"Yes!" It was a chorus.

"So we've got a dog. And they gave me a ten-buck bonus when they paid me for that job at the truck garage. So tomorrow we take off again."

"To Florida?" the older girl asked.

"What's the hurry, Jen? We'll get to Florida, one of these days."

"I thought we were going to Arizona this winter," Rusty said.

"Well, some time. California too. And Texas. Lots of places we haven't been yet."

"If anybody's hungry," Mom said, "dinner's ready."

"I'm starved," Bill said. "Come on, kids. Come on, Dog."

They all went inside, and Penny was aware that the trailer smelled of feet, bare feet. But clean bare feet. It also smelled of soap and shaving cream and cooked food. She looked around and found a sweater that had slid off a chair in the corner. It smelled like Rusty, so she lay down beside it and waited. They were the kind of people who would see to it that she had her meal in due time. And she was going to show, right to start with, that she knew her manners.

Mom looked at her and said, "Now that's the kind of a dog I like. She's had some upbringing. Help yourselves to the meatballs, but leave a couple for her."

"Her name isn't Her," Rusty declared. "Her name is Slobbers!"

"That," Jen said, wrinkling her nose, "is a disgusting name."

Mom said, "I'd give a pretty penny to know who she is and where she came from."

And Jen exclaimed, "Mom! You just named her! Let's call her Pretty Penny."

Penny thumped the floor with her tail, then stretched out comfortably with her muzzle on her paws.

Fifteen ∽

Those were the stories we told each other. Both were made of whole cloth, of course, and my fantasy was as sentimental as Barbara's romance. Both had happy endings, of a sort, because, I suppose, we both wanted that exasperating little bundle of stubborn individuality to find whatever it was she was looking for. Naturally we interpreted that goal

184

in our own terms, since we were unable to make more than a wild guess at what went on in that canine headful of instincts, emotions and thoughts.

We talked about this from time to time in the weeks that followed. We agreed that an intelligent dog, such as Penny, could follow our human trains of thought through a considerable range, but that there were barriers that limited our ability to share a dog's thinking. Or even to know whether a dog remembers yesterday or thinks ahead to tomorrow. I am quite sure about memory, but I have my doubts about anticipation.

The dog undoubtedly was the first animal tamed by prehistoric man. He dwelt with man in the caves, he was man's hunting companion in forays across the ancient plains, he was man's beast of burden pulling a small travois laden with pots and supplies on the long migrations. The dog became so domesticated, so absorbed into man's way of life, that he would fight his own kind to protect his master. He learned man's moods, his temper, his tones of voice, even his language, up to a point.

But beyond the obvious and elementary expressions, man never learned a great deal from the dog.

I have known bright dogs and stupid dogs, and even the stupid ones eventually learned enough to live comfortably with my moods and whims. The bright ones went far enough beyond that to respond to simple conversations as though they sensed what I was trying to tell them. But never was I able to reverse that process. I never learned to read the look in a dog's eyes as he lay staring at the fire on a winter hearth. I never knew what went on in his brain when he sat

185

in the dooryard and watched the river, or merely sat and
stared, deep in his own kind of meditation. I still wonder
what goes on in that mysterious dog brain when he yips and
twitches in his sleep. Pat did it often here in my study, and
when I woke him with a word he would blink and look at
me sheepishly, as though he had been far off in some secret
Somewhere that I could not enter even if I would. I said
Pat was dreaming of a rabbit chase, but that was no more
than an obvious guess. When Penny growled in her sleep
and her legs twitched, how could I know what dragons
dwelt in her dreams?

"Penny," I said, "could live in our world, but we never had
more than the most fleeting glimpse of her world."

"Perhaps that was part of the answer," Barbara said. "We
don't know what she was looking for. Even Sybil, with all
her dog knowledge, didn't know either."

We agreed that Penny demanded freedom. That was obvious. The freedom to come and go at her own whim. She
was asserting that freedom when she came to us, and when
she left us from time to time. With Sybil, she soon made it
a condition of her membership in the household. And apparently she asserted her free status everywhere she went
for a meal or a brief visit. She came and went as she pleased.
That is why Sybil called her a "free soul."

"Any dog worth remembering," I said, "also has an innate
sense of dignity, of self-respect and importance."

"That sounds stuffy," Barbara said. "I want a sense of fun,
too."

"Self-respect doesn't rule that out. By dignity I meant—
well, take the dog whose dignity is gone, whose self-respect
has been totally destroyed. He is a scuttling, cringing out-

cast. Even his own kind despise him. Yet such an outcast can be redeemed by trust and affection. I've seen it happen —a few warm meals, a home, a companion who thinks his mutt is a wonderful dog, and that dog regains self-respect. On the other hand, a proud dog can be humiliated by a length of dog chain. It probably is less a matter of lost freedom than of the indignity of being made a prisoner."

"Penny certainly hated a chain. When you chained her up, she glared at you, her tail drooped, she was utterly dejected."

"Yet she didn't mind the leash."

"She practically strutted when she was on the leash. She might try to pull your arm off, but not because she wanted to escape. She wasn't a prisoner, on a leash. She was more like a drum majorette leading a parade."

One morning over coffee Barbara said, "I can understand why she left Carol's and Tom's. And even why she was restless here—things were pretty quiet here except when she made things happen. But why should she run away and not come back at Sybil's? She had freedom, and she had what you call self-respect."

"I'm not sure she ran away," I said. "In your version of what happened, she was coming back when she was kidnapped. Anyway, Sybil's was just a kind of area headquarters. She had a bed and a meal at any one of a dozen other places whenever she wanted it. And there were all those other dogs at Sybil's, house dogs, content to stay put. Penny was a misfit among them. She wasn't one of the gang."

"Penny wasn't a one-of-the-gang dog. I still wonder where she went."

"I told you my wildest guess."

"That she was hit by a car. But they never found her body."

"Of course not. The ambulance took her to the hospital, and—"

"Yes, yes. And she went off to dog heaven on a pink cloud. I still say somebody would have found her if she'd been hit by a car."

"All right, so she wasn't hit. She was kidnapped, and drugged, and escaped. And after many harrowing adventures she found a trailer family and was welcomed with open arms to life on the open road. But the truth is that you don't know, and I don't know. Nobody knows what happened to her. And if she was just another mutt we wouldn't care."

"But we *do* care. Why? What was there about her that makes us remember?"

"You tell me. I remember cows and road trucks and sweepers. All that nonsense."

Barbara smiled. "I remember the way she looked at me that evening I let her in the first time. Her self-assurance, her confidence that she would be welcome. Her belief in a good world, a happy life. There she was, a little bit of a dog, turning to me, a total stranger, and practically saying, Hello, friend. You look like a nice person. I like you. You are going to like me."

"Yes," I agreed, "that's one thing you could count on. Penny was the equal—at least the equal—of anyone, or anything, she met. Even a highway truck."

Barbara shook her head. "You still—"

"No, I don't. I agree with you absolutely. But she did think she could stop a truck. She proved it! . . . Really, I remember her because she was so totally the individual, herself. And, as you say, because she loved life, believed in it."

The weeks became months. Snow came, and ice, and Christmas. Groundhog Day passed, and it was still winter. Now and then the red fox or his vixen, who live in a den above the old railroad right-of-way, came down near the house and barked in the night. One night they came and wakened me, they were so close. I got up to look and saw the vixen lope away, but the fox was right there in the driveway. There was a moon half past the full, and the snow made an eerie half-daylight. He stood there, watching the house, then barked, that hoarse, rasping bark we always recognize. I had a strange feeling that he was trying to say something, but I couldn't understand. He trotted off and I went back to bed, thinking of Penny, thinking what an uproar she would make if she were here.

Then it was March again. Spring peepers began to yelp and the redwing blackbirds were in the willows. An early spring, for a change. It was almost Barbara's birthday.

She came downstairs that morning, in her robe, and went to the front door and looked out, stood there several minutes before she turned away. She came into the library, then, where I was reading over my second cup of coffee, and she said, "I dreamed she came back. She didn't, did she? She's not here?"

"No."

"It was so real, I had to go look on the porch. She came back and came to the door and barked. You're sure?"

"Positive."

She brought her coffee and sat down across the table from me. "She was older. The puppy look was all gone. She looked sad. And then she saw us—we let her in—and she was Penny! Dear, bouncy Penny, tickled to death to see us." She sighed. "Don't you ever dream about her?"

"No. But I've heard her barking several times. Up on the mountain."

"When was this?"

"Oh, every now and then. The last time was a week or so ago."

"You didn't tell me."

"No."

"Why?"

"Well, the first time I heard her she turned into a barred owl. The next time she turned into a great horned owl. Then she turned into a fox. The last time she just turned into the wind, I guess."

She nodded, understanding.

Nothing more was said about Penny till after supper that evening. Then Barbara said, "I think I'll call Sybil."

"Tell her about your dream?"

"No, I just want to ask if she has heard anything. Anything at all."

She called and they talked ten or fifteen minutes. Then she came to the living room where I was half asleep in the big lounge chair. I roused and asked, "Well?"

"No word. Not a thing. She simply vanished. Sybil said everyone knew Penny, for miles around, and she would have heard if anything had happened to her. Somebody would have told her."

"Did you tell her about your dream?"

"No. But Sybil said *she* keeps waking up in the middle of the night, thinking she hears Penny bark. 'I go to the

window,' she said, 'and I look and look. But Penny isn't
there. I miss her,' she said. 'I just hope she found whatever
it was she was looking for, somewhere.'"

"Well," I said, "I guess that's that."

We sat silent, and I thought I heard something, turned to
listen. After a moment I said, "The wind. Just the wind."

But Barbara went to the front door and turned on the
porch light. She stood there looking, and after a minute or so
I got up and joined her. The big maples across the road
were still bare, but their buds were beginning to swell.
Beyond them the river glistened in the beam from the
floodlight that shone on the driveway and on across the road.
You could see down that tunnel of light into the darkness
of the night.

Barbara said, "I hope she and Saint Pat have a good time
together."

"Or she and Rusty," I said. "A dog needs a boy."

**This book may be kept
FOURTEEN DAYS**
A fine will be charged for each
day the book is kept overtime.

APR 12 '7			
Harmon			

44628